THE
breads
COOKBOOK

A SOUTHERN LIVING BOOK

contents

preface

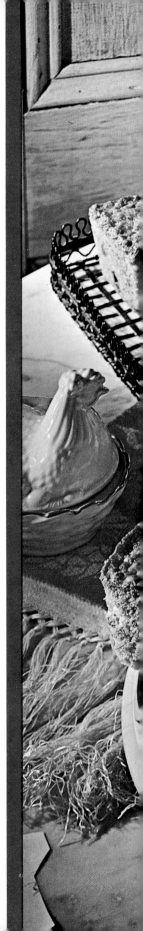

There are few more satisfying culinary experiences than preparing homemade bread. You begin with raw ingredients and by your skill in mixing, kneading, and shaping, you create unforgettable fresh-baked rolls, loaves, coffee cakes, or the much-loved waffles and pancakes.

Southern women have long taken pride in their skill as bread makers. No occasion is complete without its selection of still-warm breads. Through generations of women who honored this tradition, an entire range of bread recipes evolved. There are the typically southern corn breads ... butter-rich coffee cakes ... flaky light biscuits ... feathery pancakes and waffles ... golden rolls ... and fragrant loaves of home-baked bread!

Now *Southern Living* homemakers proudly share with you their finest bread recipes – those dependable breads that they serve when perfect flavor, exquisite texture, and eye-drawing color are all-important. As you browse through the pages that follow, imagine the pleasure you'll feel when your husband proudly announces that his wife bakes her own bread!

Everything you'll need for successful bread baking is yours in this complete *Breads Cookbook,* from home-tested, family-approved recipes to detailed editorial information. Now, from our kitchens to yours, welcome to the wonderful world of breads – southern style!

What's more exciting for a homemaker than treating her family to breads she has baked herself? Yet many homemakers deny themselves this pleasure, considering bread baking too intricate an art for them to master.

Bread making is simplicity itself. Most bread recipes are based on combinations of four major ingredients: flour, salt, liquid (including eggs), and a leavening agent. The type of leavening used determines in which of two categories bread belongs. There are *quick breads* which use baking powder, soda, air, sourdough, or steam for rising. These breads are called "quick" because they do not require a prolonged period of rising before being cooked — all the leavening takes place in the oven during baking.

In contrast to quick breads are the *yeast breads,* which rise through the action of yeast reacting upon the other ingredients. These breads require at

bread making

METHODS AND BAKING STEPS

least one period of rising before baking, and recipes for yeast breads frequently call for kneading as well.

Quick breads are readily prepared by simply following the recipe directions. However, yeast breads require some specialized knowledge — and that's what this section is all about.

YEAST BREAD INGREDIENTS

Yeast is one of the four principal ingredients in bread. It is available in cakes or in dry form. The latter is easier to store and keeps longer than cake yeast. Dry yeast is best dissolved in water that is warm but not hot when tested on your wrist; cake yeast reacts best in water which feels slightly cool to the touch.

The *liquid* in which yeast is dissolved is generally water, but some recipes specify that other liquid be added before the mixing begins. Milk is often specified because it helps create the tender, small-crumbed bread so highly prized by bread bakers. Potato water is another often-used liquid.

Flours range in type from enriched to rye or corn. The basic flour for bread making is all-purpose flour. Always be certain that the flour you buy is the best available and has been enriched — this means that the nutrients which were ground out during the milling process have been reintroduced into the flour. Serving enriched bread helps ensure that your family is getting the vitamins and minerals it needs. Many recipes specify a mixture of enriched flour with rye, corn, or whole wheat flours. The usual proportion is 80 per cent of enriched to 20 per cent of other flour. This mixture permits the bread to rise properly. The many possible combinations also allow the homemaker a wide range of bread types and flavors with which to experiment.

Salt is added to bread doughs for extra flavor and to help the rising process. It is important to never mix salt directly with the yeast or to add it to the yeast and water mixture. Salt should be dissolved with milk or other liquids before adding.

Two other ingredients are often added to yeast breads: shortening and sugar. *Shortening* helps create a loaf or roll which breaks and crushes easily and has a soft, velvety crumb. Moreover, bread which has shortening among its ingredients stays fresh longer. *Sugar* provides an immediate source of food for the yeast and helps start the rising action. It also introduces a sweet flavor to the bread and forms a golden color on the crust.

METHODS OF PREPARATION FOR YEAST BREADS

There are three frequently used methods of preparing yeast breads. The oldest is the *sponge method* in which the yeast, water, and some of the flour are combined and allowed to sit overnight. The yeast begins fermenting during this period. The remaining ingredients are added the next day; the dough is kneaded and allowed to rise according to the recipe directions.

The *straight or regular method* combines yeast with water. Then the milk (scalded), shortening, sugar, and salt are mixed in a separate container. These ingredients are then combined with the yeast and water mixture, and flour is added. Kneading follows the mixing of the dough, and there are usually two risings — one in the bowl and the other in the pans.

The *batter method* is a relatively new way of preparing bread. After the yeast is dissolved in water, ingredients are mixed in one operation and beaten with an electric mixer or by hand until they are thoroughly blended. The batter is then spooned into baking pans and allowed to rise. There is just this one rising step with batter method breads.

STEPS IN MAKING YEAST BREADS

Mixing is the beginning of bread making. You'll probably mix the yeast with water, to dissolve it. While the yeast is dissolving, scald the milk (if you're using it). Carefully note whether the recipe states that you sift the flour *before* or *after* measuring. Follow the recipe instructions carefully. Blend any other dry ingredients your recipe calls for with the flour and combine this mixture with the liquid. The mixing of your batter or dough can be done with your hand, a spoon — preferably a wooden one — or a kitchen mixer. Whatever your choice, mix *thoroughly*! Part of the success of bread making comes from the even distribution of ingredients throughout every part of the baked product.

Kneading follows mixing and is necessary in most yeast bread recipes to spread the gluten (that substance in flour which expands under the action of yeast) throughout the dough and to thoroughly blend the ingredients. You can use a pastry board, a large block, or a piece of paper on your countertop as a working surface. Flour the surface, place the dough on it, and have the remainder of your flour close at hand. Work the dough with your hands, incorporating more flour as necessary to keep the dough from becoming very sticky. But be careful: too much flour will make a coarse-textured bread.

The most effective way to knead is to use the heel of your hand — the muscle below your thumb and just above your wrist — to push the dough back and forth. To begin, flatten the dough. Then fold it in thirds from one side to the other, flatten it again, and fold it in thirds once more, this time from top to bottom. Continuing this folding-flattening process, add more flour as necessary. The process is completed when the dough is smooth and small bubbles begin to appear under the surface.

Let the kneaded dough rest while you grease a clean bowl with liquid shortening (it adheres more evenly to the bread's surface than do solid shortenings). Place the dough in the bowl, let it rest for a moment, then turn the dough over so that the greased side is up. Cover the bowl with a clean cloth, and put it in a warm place to allow the dough to rise.

Rising is a result of the interaction of gluten and yeast. It occurs best in a draftless place where the temperature is between 83 and 90 degrees. One of the best places may be in your turned-off oven — but be certain to leave the door open so gases can escape. After the time your recipe specifies for rising, press two fingers into the dough. If the dents remain, then the dough is ready for shaping.

Directions for *shaping* rolls are given in your recipe. Shaping loaves is an important factor in their final appearance. Roll the amount of dough you need for one loaf into a ball. Flatten it into a rectangle with your hands or a rolling pin, being careful to squeeze out as many gas bubbles as possible. If you're using your hands, fold the dough into thirds along the long side. Roll the dough into a loaf shape, tucking in the ends. Place it in a greased pan, seam side down. If you're using a rolling pin, roll the dough out and then roll it up as you would a jelly roll, beginning at the shorter side. Shape and place in your pan with the seam side down.

Baking usually follows a second rising of the shaped dough. Baked loaves are crusty on the outside — you can determine whether or not they are done by tapping the crust. A hollow noise indicates that baking is completed. Bread should be removed from its pan and thoroughly cooled before cutting.

For a crisp outer crust, let baked breads cool undisturbed. If your family prefers a softer crust, glaze the just-baked bread with butter and cover it for a few minutes with a clean cloth or paper towel.

Rolls turn pale gold when they are cooked. They should be served piping hot.

Breads, like so many other foods, profit from the judicious use of seasonings. You can use herbs and spices to highlight the flavors of the breads you serve and to complement the main course. With imagination you can create breads for any occasion, and you'll soon find yourself serving fragrant warm breads and rolls to enhance every meal.

Just think what you can do with the plain baking powder biscuit. Add grated cheese to your dough, and you have cheese biscuits to match a meat loaf or other ground beef dish. Other variations are possible with minced parsley — always a good addition to breads — chopped onion or pimento, or cinnamon-and-sugar toppings. Experiment and develop a repertoire of seasoned breads for every occasion.

The following list of seasonings suggests some of the possible combinations you may want to try:

seasonings
FOR BREADS

Caraway seeds are called for in many recipes both as seasonings and as toppings. They are particularly good in breads made with whole grains, such as oatmeal. Caraway seeds, like other seeds, should be stored in the refrigerator to prevent their becoming rancid.

Celery seed has a mild and piquant flavor which adds greatly to the flavor of whole grain breads. Try a pinch in the next bread you bake, and serve with a casserole supper. The meal becomes an adventure in great eating!

Chervil is one of the most versatile of all herbs and is a staple seasoning of French cookery. Try a pinch of this parsley-like herb in your next corn bread. You'll be amazed at how delicious it tastes.

Chive is a mild-flavored member of the onion family. Try adding it to cheese and garlic bread doughs or to the dumplings you prepare for chicken or beef stew.

Cinnamon is a spice featured in rolls, coffee cakes, and even in waffles and pancakes. It is often mixed with sugar in a four parts sugar to one part cinnamon mixture and used as a topping for French toast, biscuits, and other quick breads.

Clove is a heady spice with a strong aroma and flavor. It should be used carefully and in combination with other spices such as nutmeg, mace, and cinnamon in sweet rolls, coffee cakes, and dessert breads.

Dill is a delightfully flavored herb and brings new excitement to biscuits or breads made with onion or cheese.

Ginger is a spice frequently used in coffee cakes or sweet rolls. Try it in your next waffle batter and enjoy a real taste treat!

Nutmeg is a spice used by itself as a topping for pancakes, French toast, or waffles or in combination with other spices in sweet rolls and coffee cakes. Add a touch of nutmeg to your herb breads — it will highlight the other seasonings.

Oregano, or wild marjoram, is an herb which is used to advantage in garlic breads or those served with Italian foods.

Parsley, an herb which provides much-needed Vitamin C, adds both flavor and color to biscuits, dumplings, herb breads, and other quick and yeast breads.

Poppy seeds are tiny dark granules with a flavor all their own. They are sprinkled on top of rolls, biscuits, and breads or may be mixed with the batter or dough for many sweet breads.

Rosemary is a delicately flavored herb often used in combination with sage or savory in dumplings or biscuits. These breads are particularly tasty served as accompaniments to poultry dishes.

Saffron is one of the most precious spices and lends a golden glow to the foods it flavors. There are saffron breads, and there are also many basic recipes to which saffron may be added for flavoring. Commercial bakers often include a pinch of saffron in their doughs to lend good color.

Sage, an herb with strong flavor, is often added to herb breads. It is almost always combined with other herbs and should be used in moderation.

Savory is an herb used in combination with others in both quick and yeast breads, especially those served with meat or poultry dishes.

Sesame seeds are sprinkled on breads, rolls, buns, and biscuits. Most recipes call for the seeds to be toasted — this can be done in your oven at low temperature. For really exciting pancakes, particularly those with a corn-meal base, add a teaspoon or two of seeds to the batter.

Thyme is another herb which is often featured in both quick and yeast breads — it's good in combination with sage or savory.

In using herbs, be certain to remember that one-quarter teaspoon of dried is equivalent to one teaspoon of fresh — make the substitution your recipe requires. And to keep seeds from turning rancid, try storing them in the refrigerator.

Happy seasoning!

Baking Powder: A leavening agent, more reliable than baking soda, which reacts with liquid to produce bubbles of carbon dioxide that are trapped in the dough or batter. This causes the mixture to rise and become light and porous. The intense oven heat then acts to stabilize this porous structure.

Baking Soda: A leavening agent of pure sodium bicarbonate which produces carbon dioxide when heated. Baking soda must be combined with an acid (present either among the food ingredients or in baking powder) to prevent the objectionable taste left by the sodium carbonate.

Batter: Any mixture of flour, moisture, and other ingredients.

Biscuit: A tender, flaky bread with a smooth, brown crust, leavened with baking powder and shaped into a small cake.

OF BAKING TERMS

Blintze: A thin pancake folded around a filling of cottage cheese, fruit or meat. It is fried until golden brown and is often served with a topping of sour cream, applesauce or jam.

Brioche: A soft, muffin-shaped roll with a small puff or knob on top, made of butter, eggs, flour, and yeast.

Buns: Individual breads, often containing candied fruits or raisins, that are molded or baked in muffin tins. They are a variation on the standard yeast bread recipe; the most famous variety is the Eastertime favorite: hot cross buns.

Buckwheat: A dark flour, obtained from the seeds of the buckwheat plant, it is most frequently used for buckwheat pancakes. To weaken its pungent flavor, buckwheat flour is usually combined with white flour.

Citron: A fruit, grown in the Mediterranean area and California, which resembles a lemon but is larger and less acid. The thick skin is candied and used in many baked products.

Coffee Cake: A rich sweet bread shaped in various ways and sometimes iced. It is usually leavened with yeast and may contain spices, nuts and fruits. Coffee cakes are often enjoyed at breakfast.

Corn Bread: A quick bread prepared from cornmeal, flour, sugar, shortening, and baking powder.

Cornmeal: Coarsely ground corn, with or without the hull and germ kernel, it is available either as yellow or white meal. It is the primary ingredient in all corn bread recipes.

Crumb: The soft inner portion of a loaf of bread, as distinguished from the crust.

Crust: The outside of a loaf of bread, formed by the intense oven heat and the consequent drying of the surface of the loaf.

Dough: The unbaked mixture of flour, water, yeast, and other ingredients. It should be stiff enough to be kneaded or worked with the hands.

Doughnut: A small, ring-shaped cake made from leavened and sweetened dough that is fried in hot shortening. Doughnuts are generally glazed, iced, dusted with sugar, or filled with jelly or custard.

Fermentation: A chemical change in organic substances caused by micro-organisms. In bread making the tiny yeast plant ferments and the carbon dioxide, which is a by-product of this change, causes the bread to rise.

Flour: The finely ground meal made from grain, usually bolted, i.e. sifted to obtain a powdery texture. *All-purpose flour* is bleached or unbleached refined wheat flour to which vitamins and minerals are usually added.

Gluten: The protein constituent of wheat and other cereals which, when combined with liquid, interacts with yeast to produce carbon dioxide. These bubbles of CO_2 are held in the dough by the elastic fibers of gluten. Kneading then stretches the fibers into a minute network, which allows the dough to expand evenly and properly.

Griddle: A heavy, flat, and often rimless metal pan that is used to make pancakes, etc.

Kolachke (Kolache, Kolachy): A yeast-raised bun that varies in sweetness and is filled with apples, prunes, figs, nuts, poppy seeds, and jam.

Loaf pan: A 9" x 5" x 3" baking pan of metal or glass which gives the baked loaves of bread their characteristic shape.

Muffins: Small and light cup-shaped breads to which nuts, fruits, jams, etc. are often added. Muffins are sometimes called gems, though there is no real difference between the two.

Muffin pan (tin): A baking pan with cup-shaped cavities into which muffin or cupcake batter is poured and baked.

Oatmeal: A meal made from ground or rolled oats that is used in baking oatmeal bread and cookies or cooked and served as a hot cereal.

Pancakes: Flat, round cakes made from a variety of batters and cooked over direct heat on a griddle, usually served for breakfast. However, when prepared from a thinner batter and wrapped around a filling, pancakes are delicious dessert treats known as crepes.

Pumpernickel: A dark bread made from either unsifted rye flour or the combination of wheat and rye flours. The dark and coarse bread made from pure rye flour may have a slight, pleasantly sour taste, while the lighter bread that contains wheat flour is milder.

Quick Breads: Breads such as biscuits, muffins, corn breads, nut-fruit breads, griddle cakes and doughnuts which are leavened with baking powder, soda, air, or steam instead of yeast. They are quick to prepare and improve their flavor in storage.

Rye flour: A dark, tasty flour which lacks gluten-forming protein. It is used in the preparation of rye and pumpernickel breads, and most frequently combined with other flours in order to produce less crumbly loaves of smooth, porous texture.

Sourdough: A clump of dough, stored in a covered container, that is a living and continuing fermentation. It is used in the preparation of leavened bread.

Sponge: The dough formed either from flour, water, yeast, and other ingredients, or from starter dough.

Starter dough: An old-fashioned method of preparing yeast breads which entails brewing a mixture of hops, water, flour, and sugar and allowing it to ferment. The mixture is then used instead of yeast to leaven batters.

Stollen: A German yeast bread baked in the form of an oval loaf. It contains almonds, candied orange and lemon peel, and currants.

Waffles: Batter cakes, crisper than pancakes, that are baked in a waffle iron. They may be served either as a breakfast food or as a dessert with ice cream or fruit.

Waffle iron: A cooking device used in the preparation of waffles that consists of two hinged, honeycomb-like metal griddles. In general, both top and bottom irons are heated by electricity.

Whole Wheat, Graham, or Wheat Flour: An unrefined flour obtained by grinding the entire wheat grain (bran, endosperm, and germ included) to a powdery consistency. Wheat flour is rich in vitamin, mineral, and roughage content, because most of the bran or outer coat is retained during milling.

Yeast: A minute vegetable substance that is activated by the proper conditions of temperature, moisture, air, and food. The result of this interaction entails the fermentation of sugar by the yeast. The essential by-products are: carbon dioxide which forms bubbles and causes the dough to expand; and alcohol which is vaporized during baking. It is available in cakes as compressed yeast or in packages of active dry yeast.

loaves & rolls

YEAST

The incomparable smell of freshly-baked bread seems to fill an entire house with a warm glow that lasts long after the baking process is ended. Southern homemakers — women who take pride in serving foods people enjoy — know that preparing homemade breads is one of the nicest things a woman can do for her friends and family. Through the years of creative bread baking, they have amassed a varied and exciting collection of yeast bread and roll recipes.

Here you'll discover recipes for Anadama Bread, that cornmeal-based bread which has played an important role not just in southern but in American cooking . . . French Bread as it is prepared along the Gulf Coast, crisp-crusted outside and tender on the inside . . . Herbed Cheese Bread, a savory blending of flavors which brings excitement to any meal . . . and many more.

Yeast rolls are featured here, too, in such recipes as Basic Refrigerator Rolls, a marvelously versatile recipe which lends itself to an infinite number of variations . . . Onion Rolls, the family favorite . . . and typically southern Fresh Potato Rolls Delicious.

These are just some of the home-tested recipes waiting for you in the pages of this section. Every recipe is the favorite of a southern homemaker . . . try one tonight, and let it become your favorite, too!

OATMEAL BANNOCKS

2 1/2 to 3 c. unsifted flour	1/2 c. milk
1/3 c. sugar	1/2 c. water
3/4 tsp. salt	1/4 c. margarine
1 c. old-fashioned rolled oats	1 egg, at room temperature
2 pkg. dry yeast	1/2 c. currants

Mix 3/4 cup flour, sugar, salt, oats and undissolved yeast thoroughly in a large bowl. Combine the milk, water and margarine in a saucepan and place over low heat until liquids are warm. Margarine does not need to melt. Add to dry ingredients gradually and beat for 2 minutes with electric mixer at medium speed, scraping bowl occasionally. Add egg and 1/2 cup flour and beat at high speed for 2 minutes, scraping bowl occasionally. Stir in enough remaining flour to make a soft dough. Turn out onto a lightly floured board and knead for 8 to 10 minutes or until smooth and elastic. Place in a greased bowl and turn to grease top. Cover and let rise in a warm place, free from draft, for about 45 minutes or until doubled in bulk. Punch down. Turn out onto a lightly floured board and knead in the currants. Divide in half and roll each half into an 8-inch circle. Place in 2 greased 8-inch round cake pans. Cut each circle into 8 wedges with a sharp knife, cutting almost through to bottom. Cover and let rise in warm place, free from draft, for about 30 minutes or until doubled in bulk. Bake in 375-degree oven for about 20 minutes or until done. Remove from pans and cool on wire racks.

Photograph for this recipe on cover.

BARM BRACK

4 1/2 to 5 1/2 c. unsifted flour	1/2 c. milk
1/2 c. sugar	1/4 c. margarine
1 1/2 tsp. salt	2 eggs, at room temperature
1 tsp. grated lemon peel	1 1/4 c. golden seedless raisins
3 pkg. dry yeast	1/3 c. chopped mixed candied fruits
3/4 c. water	

Mix 1 1/2 cups flour, sugar, salt, lemon peel and undissolved yeast thoroughly in a large bowl. Combine the water, milk and margarine in a saucepan and place over low heat until liquids are warm. Margarine does not need to melt. Add to dry ingredients gradually and beat for 2 minutes with electric mixer at medium speed, scraping bowl occasionally. Add the eggs and 3/4 cup flour and beat at high speed for 2 minutes, scraping bowl occasionally. Stir in enough remaining flour to make a soft dough. Turn out onto a lightly floured board and knead for 8 to 10 minutes or until smooth and elastic. Place in a greased bowl and turn to grease top. Cover and let rise in a warm place, free from draft, for about 40 minutes or until doubled in bulk. Punch down. Turn out onto a lightly floured board and knead in raisins and candied fruits. Divide in half. Shape into loaves. Place in 2 greased 8 1/2 x 4 1/2 x 2 1/2-inch loaf pans. Cover and let rise in a warm place, free from draft, for about 50 minutes or until doubled in bulk. Bake in 375-degree oven for 30 to 35 minutes or until done. Remove from pans and cool on wire racks.

Photograph for this recipe on cover.

ONION BREAD

1 c. milk, scalded	2 pkg. yeast
3 tbsp. sugar	3/4 c. warm water
1 tbsp. salt	1/2 c. chopped onion
1 1/2 tbsp. oil	6 c. flour

Mix the milk, sugar, salt and oil in a bowl and cool to lukewarm. Dissolve the yeast in warm water, then stir into milk mixture. Add the onion and 4 cups flour and mix well. Add remaining flour, small amount at a time, beating well after each addition. Cover and let rise for 45 minutes. Punch down and place in 2 greased loaf pans. Let rise until doubled in bulk. Bake at 350 degrees for 1 hour.

Mrs. Robert Kurz, Charleston, South Carolina

SPICED RYE LOAVES

3 pkg. yeast	1 tbsp. vinegar
1/4 c. melted butter or margarine	2 tbsp. caraway seed
2 1/2 c. lukewarm milk or water	4 c. rye flour
2 tsp. salt	4 c. (about) flour
6 tbsp. molasses or corn syrup	

Place the yeast in a bowl. Mix the butter and milk. Pour over the yeast and stir until dissolved. Add the salt, molasses, vinegar and caraway seed and mix. Add the rye flour and half the flour and mix well. Add enough remaining flour to make a stiff dough and mix well. Let rise until doubled in bulk. Stir down and place in 2 greased and floured loaf pans. Let rise until doubled in bulk. Bake in 325-degree oven for about 1 hour. Brush with water. Remove from pans and cool on wire rack. One tablespoon aniseed or grated orange rind may be substituted for caraway seed.

ANADAMA BREAD

1 pkg. yeast	2 tbsp. shortening
1/2 c. warm water	1/2 c. molasses
1/2 c. yellow cornmeal	2 tbsp. salt
2 c. boiling water	6 c. all-purpose flour

Dissolve the yeast in warm water. Stir the cornmeal into boiling water slowly. Stir in the shortening, molasses and salt and cool to lukewarm. Stir in the yeast, then the flour and beat until smooth. Knead on a floured surface for 8 to 10 minutes or until smooth and elastic. Place in a greased bowl and turn to grease surface. Cover and let rise for about 1 hour and 30 minutes or until doubled in bulk. Punch down, then let rise for 10 minutes. Shape into 2 loaves and place in loaf pans. Let rise for about 1 hour or until doubled in bulk. Bake at 400 degrees for 50 minutes to 1 hour. Remove from pans and cool on a rack.

Mrs. Charles V. Horn, Hereford, Texas

BUTTERMILK BREAD

1 c. buttermilk	1 pkg. yeast
3 tbsp. sugar	1 c. warm water
2 1/2 tsp. salt	5 1/2 to 5 3/4 c. flour
1/3 c. shortening	1/4 tsp. soda

Scald the buttermilk in a saucepan. Stir in sugar, salt and shortening and cool to lukewarm. Sprinkle the yeast over warm water in a mixing bowl and stir until dissolved. Stir in the buttermilk mixture. Add 3 cups flour and soda and beat until smooth. Add enough remaining flour to make a stiff dough. Turn out onto a lightly floured board and knead for about 10 minutes or until smooth and elastic. Place in a greased bowl and cover with a cloth. Let rise in a warm place for about 1 hour or until doubled in bulk. Punch down. Place on a lightly floured cloth and let rest for 15 minutes. Cut in half and place in 2 loaf pans. Cover and let rise in a warm place for about 1 hour or until center is slightly higher than pan. Bake at 400 degrees for 45 minutes.

Mrs. R. A. Aldridge, Gretna, Virginia

MIXED BREAD

1 pkg. dry yeast	1/4 c. shortening
1 c. lukewarm water	2 tbsp. sugar
4 c. unsifted flour	2 tsp. salt
1 c. cooked cold grits	Soft butter or margarine

Dissolve the yeast in water. Mix the flour, grits, shortening, sugar and salt in a bowl and stir in the yeast. Knead on a floured surface until smooth and elastic. Place in a well-greased loaf pan and grease top with butter. Let rise until doubled in bulk. Bake at 400 degrees for 45 to 50 minutes or until light brown. Remove from pan and place loaf on oven rack. Bake until golden brown. Remove from oven and brush top of loaf with butter.

Mrs. B. W. Crouch, McCormick, South Carolina

CHEESE-HERB BUFFET LOAVES

6 to 7 c. unsifted flour	1/2 c. grated Parmesan cheese
2 tbsp. sugar	1/2 c. finely chopped parsley
2 tsp. salt	1/2 tsp. oregano leaves
2 pkg. dry yeast	1/2 tsp. garlic salt
1 c. milk	1 egg white, slightly beaten
1/4 c. margarine	

Mix 2 cups flour, sugar, salt and undissolved yeast thoroughly in a large bowl. Combine the milk, 1 cup water and margarine in a saucepan and place over low heat until liquids are warm. Margarine does not need to melt. Add to dry ingredients gradually and beat for 2 minutes with electric mixer at medium speed, scraping bowl occasionally. Add 3/4 cup flour and beat at high speed for 2 minutes, scraping bowl occasionally. Stir in enough remaining flour to make a soft dough. Turn out onto a lightly floured board and knead for 8 to 10 minutes or until smooth and elastic. Place in a greased bowl and turn to grease top. Cover and let rise in a warm place, free from draft, for about 30 minutes or until doubled in bulk. Combine cheese, parsley, oregano and garlic salt. Punch dough down. Turn out onto a lightly floured board and divide in half. Let rest for 5 minutes. Roll out 1/2 of the dough into 8 x 15-inch rectangle. Sprinkle with half the cheese mixture. Cut into three 8 x 5-inch rectangles and roll each rectangle from 8-inch side as for jelly roll. Pinch seams to seal. Pinch ends and fold underneath. Place loaves, seam side down and 1/4 inch apart, on half of a greased baking sheet. Repeat with remaining dough and filling and place loaves on same baking sheet. Cover and let rise in a warm place, free from draft, for about 30 minutes or until doubled in bulk. Bake in 400-degree oven for 10 minutes, then remove from oven. Mix the egg white with 2 tablespoons water and brush on loaves. Sprinkle with sesame seed, if desired. Bake for 15 minutes longer or until done. Remove from baking sheet and cool on wire rack. Separate loaves and slice each into 1/2-inch slices. Seasoned salt may be substituted for garlic salt.

FRENCH BREAD

2 c. warm water	5 3/4 to 6 c. flour
1 pkg. dry yeast	1 egg white
2 tbsp. sugar	Sesame or poppy seed (opt.)
2 tsp. salt	

Pour the warm water into a bowl. Sprinkle yeast over water and stir until dissolved. Add the sugar, salt and 3 cups flour and stir until mixed. Stir in 2 1/2 cups flour. Sprinkle remaining flour on a bread board. Turn dough out onto flour and knead for 5 to 10 minutes or until smooth. Shape into a ball and place in a greased bowl. Cover and let rise until doubled in bulk. Divide in half, cover and let stand for 5 minutes. Shape into 2 long loaves with tapered ends. Place loaves 4 inches apart on a lightly greased baking sheet. Cut diagonal slits about 3/4 inch deep and 1 1/2 inches apart into top of each loaf. Cover and let rise for about 1 hour or until doubled in bulk. Brush tops with egg white and sprinkle with sesame seed. Bake at 400 degrees for 5 minutes and remove from oven. Brush loaves with cold water. Reduce temperature to 350 degrees and bake for 25 minutes longer.

Mrs. Ellsworth Hay, Noble County, Oklahoma

HERBED CHEESE BREAD

1 c. milk	1/2 c. warm water
1/4 c. butter or margarine	1/4 c. grated Romano cheese
1 1/2 tbsp. sugar	1/2 c. grated Parmesan cheese
1 1/2 tsp. salt	1/2 tsp. oregano
1 egg, slightly beaten	1/4 tsp. marjoram
1 pkg. dry yeast	4 1/2 c. sifted flour

Scald the milk in a medium saucepan over low heat. Stir in the butter, sugar and salt until melted. Remove from heat and cool to lukewarm. Stir in the egg. Dissolve the yeast in warm water in a medium mixing bowl. Add the milk mixture and mix. Stir in the cheeses, oregano and marjoram. Stir in 1 cup flour and beat until smooth. Stir in remaining flour, 1 cup at a time, beating well after each addition. Turn onto board sprinkled with remaining flour and knead until smooth and elastic. Place in a large mixing bowl. Cover and let rise in a warm place for about 1 hour or until doubled in bulk. Turn onto a well-floured board and roll with a floured rolling pin until all air bubbles are gone. Fold into a smooth loaf and place in a well-greased 9 x 5 x 3-inch loaf pan. Cover and let rise in a warm place for about 45 minutes or until top is well rounded. Bake in 400-degree oven for 50 minutes or until golden brown. Remove from oven and turn out of pan immediately. Cool at room temperature.

Mrs. James F. Dorsey, Arkadelphia, Arkansas

HOMEMADE LIGHT BREAD

1 c. milk	2 1/2 tsp. salt
3 tbsp. sugar	6 tbsp. shortening

1 pkg. dry yeast
1 c. warm water

6 c. sifted flour
Melted shortening

Scald the milk and stir in sugar, salt and shortening until sugar is dissolved. Cool to lukewarm. Sprinkle yeast on water in a bowl and stir until dissolved. Add milk mixture. Stir in 3 cups flour and beat until smooth. Stir in remaining flour. Turn out on a lightly floured board and knead until smooth and elastic. Place in a greased bowl and brush top with melted shortening. Cover with a damp cloth and let rise in a warm place for about 1 hour or until doubled in bulk. Punch down and place in 2 greased 8 x 4 x 3-inch loaf pans. Cover with a damp cloth and let rise in a warm place for about 1 hour or until center of dough is slightly higher than top of the pans. Bake at 400 degrees for 50 minutes to 1 hour. Remove from pans immediately and cool on a rack.

Jessie Steakley, Lepanto, Arkansas

HEALTH BUNS

1 pkg. yeast
1/4 c. melted butter or
     margarine
2 c. lukewarm skim milk
1 tbsp. molasses or corn syrup

2 tsp. salt
2 3/4 c. whole wheat flour
2 3/4 to 3 1/4 c. flour
1 3/4 c. graham flour

Place the yeast in a bowl. Mix the butter and skim milk. Pour over yeast and stir until dissolved. Add the molasses, salt, whole wheat flour, 2 3/4 cups flour and graham flour and mix well. Add enough remaining flour to make a stiff dough. Let rise until doubled in bulk. Knead on lightly floured surface until smooth and elastic, then shape into oblong buns. Place on a greased baking sheet and let rise until doubled in bulk. Bake at 400 degrees for 10 to 15 minutes.

OLD-FASHIONED WHOLE WHEAT LOAVES

4 1/2 c. unsifted whole wheat flour	**2 pkg. dry yeast**
2 3/4 c. (about) unsifted flour	**1 1/2 c. water**
3 tbsp. sugar	**3/4 c. milk**
4 tsp. salt	**1/3 c. molasses**
	1/3 c. margarine

Combine the flours. Mix 2 1/2 cups flour mixture, sugar, salt and undissolved yeast thoroughly in a large bowl. Combine the water, milk, molasses and margarine in a saucepan and place over low heat until liquids are warm. Margarine does not need to melt. Add to dry ingredients gradually and beat for 2 minutes with electric mixer at medium speed, scraping sides of bowl occasionally. Add 1/2 cup flour mixture and beat at high speed for 2 minutes, scraping bowl occasionally. Stir in enough remaining flour mixture to make a soft dough. Turn out onto a lightly floured board and knead for 8 to 10 minutes or until smooth and elastic. Place in a greased bowl and turn to grease top. Cover and let rise in a warm place, free from draft, for about 1 hour or until doubled in bulk. Punch down. Turn out onto a lightly floured board and divide into 4 equal pieces. Form each piece into a round ball and place on greased baking sheets. Cover and let rise in a warm place, free from draft, for about 1 hour or until doubled in bulk. Bake in 400-degree oven for about 25 minutes or until done. Remove from baking sheets and cool on wire racks.

ONE-BOWL HARD ROLLS

4 1/2 to 5 1/2 c. unsifted flour	**1 egg white, at room temperature**
2 tbsp. sugar	**Cornmeal**
2 tsp. salt	**1/2 c. water**
1 pkg. yeast	**1 tsp. cornstarch**
3 tbsp. softened margarine	
1 1/2 c. hot tap water	

Mix 1 1/3 cups flour, sugar, salt and undissolved yeast thoroughly in a bowl. Add softened margarine. Add hot water to dry ingredients gradually and beat for 2 minutes with electric mixer at medium speed, scraping bowl occasionally. Add the egg white and 1 cup flour and beat at high speed for 2 minutes, scraping bowl occasionally. Stir in enough additional flour to make a soft dough. Turn out onto a lightly floured board and knead for 8 to 10 minutes or until smooth and elastic. Place in a greased bowl and turn to grease top. Cover and let rise in a warm place, free from draft, for about 45 minutes or until doubled in bulk. Punch down and turn out onto a lightly floured board. Cover and let rest for 10 minutes. Divide in half and form each half into a 9-inch roll. Cut into nine 1-inch pieces and form into smooth balls. Place about 3 inches apart on greased baking sheets sprinkled with cornmeal. Cover and let rise in a warm place, free from draft for about 45 minutes or until doubled in bulk. Blend water into cornstarch in a saucepan. Bring to a boil, then cool slightly. Brush each roll with cornstarch glaze and slit tops crisscross fashion with a sharp knife. Sprinkle with sesame or poppy seed, if desired. Bake in a 450-degree oven for about 15 minutes or until done. Remove from baking sheets and cool on wire racks.

Photograph for this recipe on page 19.

BASIC REFRIGERATOR ROLLS

2 c. boiling water	2 pkg. yeast
1/2 c. shortening	1/2 c. warm water
1/2 c. sugar	6 c. unsifted flour
1 tbsp. salt	

Mix the boiling water, shortening, sugar and salt in a bowl and cool to lukewarm. Dissolve the yeast in the warm water. Add to the sugar mixture and mix well. Stir in the flour and grease the top and cover. Let rise in a warm place until doubled in bulk. Punch down and cover. Place in refrigerator until ready to bake. Roll out on a floured surface and cut with a biscuit cutter. Fold over and place on a greased cookie sheet. Let rise until doubled in bulk. Bake in a 400-degree oven for 15 minutes. 3 dozen.

Mrs. Dick Wilson, Joiner, Arkansas

YEAST ROLLS

1 pkg. dry yeast	1 1/2 tbsp. shortening
1/4 c. sugar	1 egg, beaten
1 tsp. salt	4 c. flour

Dissolve the yeast and 1/2 teaspoon sugar in 1/4 cup lukewarm water in a large mixing bowl. Add remaining sugar, salt, shortening, egg and 1 cup warm water and mix well. Stir in 2 cups flour, then stir in remaining flour. Place in refrigerator until ready to use. Shape into rolls and place on a greased baking sheet. Let rise for 1 hour and 30 minutes or until doubled in bulk. Bake in 425-degree oven until browned. 18 rolls.

Mrs. Willie Chance, Elizabeth, Louisiana

ONE-BOWL DINNER ROLLS

2 3/4 to 3 1/4 c. unsifted flour	5 tbsp. softened margarine
1/4 c. sugar	2/3 c. hot tap water
1/2 tsp. salt	1 egg, at room temperature
1 pkg. dry yeast	Melted margarine

Mix 3/4 cup flour, sugar, salt and undissolved yeast thoroughly in a large bowl. Add softened margarine. Add the hot water gradually and beat for 2 minutes with electric mixer at medium speed, scraping bowl occasionally. Add egg and 1/2 cup flour and beat at high speed for 2 minutes, scraping bowl occasionally. Stir in enough remaining flour to make a soft dough. Turn out onto a lightly floured board and knead for 8 to 10 minutes or until smooth and elastic. Place in a greased bowl and turn to grease top. Cover and let rise in a warm place, free from draft, for about 1 hour or until doubled in bulk. Punch down. Turn out onto a lightly floured board. Divide into 2 equal pieces. Divide each piece into 12 pieces. Roll each into a pencil-shaped 16-inch roll. Shape into pretzels and place about 2 inches apart on greased baking sheets. Cover and let rise in a warm place, free from draft, for about 1 hour or until doubled in bulk. Brush with melted margarine. Bake in a 400-degree oven for 10 to 15 minutes or until done. Remove from baking sheets and cool on wire racks. May be shaped into Parker House or curlicue rolls.

Photograph for this recipe on page 2.

FRESH POTATO ROLLS DELICIOUS

1 pkg. dry yeast	2 tsp. salt
1/2 c. warm water	3 lge. eggs, lightly beaten
2/3 c. scalded milk	8 1/2 c. (about) sifted flour
1/2 c. shortening	3 tbsp. melted butter or margarine
1 c. fresh hot mashed potatoes	
1/4 c. sugar	

Sprinkle the yeast over warm water and stir until dissolved. Combine the milk, shortening, potatoes, sugar and salt in a large bowl and cool to lukewarm. Add the yeast and eggs and blend well. Add 1 1/2 cups flour and mix well. Cover and let rise in a warm place for about 1 hour or until bubbly. Stir in enough remaining flour to make a stiff dough. Turn onto a lightly floured board and knead until smooth and elastic. Place in a lightly greased bowl and turn to grease surface. Cover and refrigerate overnight. Shape into small balls. Place in greased and lightly floured muffin tins and brush with melted butter. Let rise in a warm place for 1 hour and 15 minutes or until doubled in bulk. Bake at 425 degrees for 20 minutes. About 40 medium rolls.

Photograph for this recipe on page 14.

SOURDOUGH BREAD

5 to 6 c. unsifted flour	1 c. milk
3 tbsp. sugar	2 tbsp. margarine
1 tsp. salt	1 1/2 c. Starter
1 pkg. dry yeast	

Combine 1 cup flour, sugar, salt and undissolved yeast in a large bowl. Combine the milk and margarine in a saucepan and place over low heat until liquid is warm. Margarine does not need to melt. Add to dry ingredients gradually and beat for 2 minutes with electric mixer at medium speed, scraping bowl occasionally. Add Starter and 1 cup flour and beat at high speed for 2 minutes, scraping bowl occasionally. Stir in enough remaining flour to make a soft dough. Turn out onto a lightly floured board and knead for 8 to 10 minutes or until smooth and elastic. Place in a greased bowl and turn to grease top. Cover and let rise in a warm place, free from draft, for about 1 hour or until doubled in bulk. Punch down. Turn out onto a lightly floured board and let rest for 15 minutes. Divide in half. Shape each half into a loaf and place in 2 greased 9 x 5 x 3-inch loaf pans. Cover and let rise in warm place, free from draft, for about 1 hour or until doubled in bulk. Bake in 400-degree oven for about 30 minutes or until done. Remove from pans and cool on wire racks.

Starter

2 1/2 c. unsifted flour	**1 tbsp. salt**
Sugar	**1 pkg. dry yeast**

Combine 1 3/4 cups flour, 1 tablespoon sugar, salt and undissolved yeast in a bowl. Add 2 1/2 cups warm water gradually and beat for 2 minutes with electric mixer at medium speed, scraping bowl occasionally. Cover and let stand at room temperature for 4 days, stirring down daily. To reuse Starter, add remaining flour, 1 1/2 teaspoons sugar and 1 1/2 cups lukewarm water and beat for 1 minute with electric mixer at medium speed. Cover and let stand until ready to make bread again, stirring down daily.

PARKER HOUSE ROLLS

2 3/4 to 3 1/4 c. unsifted flour	5 tbsp. softened margarine
1/4 c. sugar	2/3 c. hot tap water
1/2 tsp. salt	1 egg, at room temperature
1 pkg. dry yeast	Melted margarine

Mix 3/4 cup flour, sugar, salt and undissolved yeast thoroughly in a large bowl. Add softened margarine. Add hot water gradually and beat for 2 minutes with electric mixer at medium speed, scraping bowl occasionally. Add the egg and 1/2 cup flour and beat at high speed for 2 minutes, scraping bowl occasionally. Stir in enough remaining flour to make a soft dough. Turn out onto a lightly floured board and knead for 8 to 10 minutes or until smooth and elastic. Place in a greased bowl and turn to grease top. Cover and let rise in a warm place, free from draft, for about 1 hour or until doubled in bulk. Punch down. Turn out onto a lightly floured board and divide in half. Roll each half into a 1/4-inch thick circle, then cut with a 2 1/2-inch biscuit cutter. Crease each round with dull edge of knife to one side of center and brush each round with melted margarine to within 1/4 inch of edge. Fold larger side over smaller so edges just meet and pinch well with fingers to seal. Place on greased baking sheets so rolls are almost touching. Cover and let rise in a warm place, free from draft, for about 1 hour or until doubled in bulk. Brush rolls with melted margarine. Bake in 400-degree oven for 10 to 15 minutes or until done. Remove from baking sheets and cool on wire racks. 2-3 dozen.

Photograph for this recipe on page 25.

TINY LEMON STICKY BUNS

4 1/2 to 5 1/2 c. unsifted flour	1 c. margarine
3 c. sugar	1 egg, at room temperature
2 tsp. salt	1 c. chopped blanched almonds
4 tbsp. grated lemon peel	1/2 c. light corn syrup
2 pkg. dry yeast	1/2 tsp. ground nutmeg
3/4 c. milk	Melted margarine

Mix 1 1/2 cups flour, 1/2 cup sugar, salt, 1 tablespoon lemon peel and undissolved yeast thoroughly in a large bowl. Combine the milk, 1/2 cup water and 1/2 cup margarine in a saucepan and place over low heat until liquids are warm. Margarine does not need to melt. Add to dry ingredients gradually and beat for 2 minutes with electric mixer at medium speed, scraping bowl occasionally. Add the egg and 1/2 cup flour and beat at high speed for 2 minutes, scraping bowl occasionally. Stir in enough remaining flour to make a soft dough. Turn out onto a lightly floured board and knead for 8 to 10 minutes or until smooth and elastic. Place in a greased bowl and turn to grease top. Cover and let rise in a warm place, free from draft, for about 1 hour or until doubled in bulk. Sprinkle the almonds into 3 greased 9-inch round cake pans. Combine 1 1/2 cups sugar, remaining margarine, corn syrup, 1/4 cup water and remaining lemon peel in a saucepan. Bring to a boil and cook for 3 minutes, stirring constantly. Pour over almonds. Combine remaining sugar and nutmeg. Punch dough down. Turn out onto a lightly floured board and divide in 3 equal pieces. Roll each piece into a 20 x 8-inch rectangle. Brush with melted margarine and sprinkle with nutmeg mixture. Roll each up from long side as for jelly roll and seal edges firmly. Cut into 1-inch slices. Place, cut side up, in prepared pans. Cover and let rise in a warm place, free from draft, for about 1 hour or until doubled in bulk. Bake in 350-degree oven for 20 to 25 minutes or until done. Invert buns onto plates or wire racks to cool. 5 dozen.

Photograph for this recipe on page 19.

SEMMELS

4 to 5 c. unsifted flour	1/4 c. potato water
1/4 c. sugar	1/4 c. margarine
1/2 tsp. salt	1 egg, at room temperature
1 pkg. dry yeast	1/4 c. warm mashed potatoes
1 c. milk	

Mix 1 cup flour, sugar, salt and undissolved yeast thoroughly in a large bowl. Combine the milk, potato water and margarine in a saucepan and place over low heat until liquids are warm. Margarine does not need to melt. Add to dry ingredients gradually and beat for 2 minutes with electric mixer at medium speed, scraping bowl occasionally. Add the egg, potatoes and 1/2 cup flour and beat at high speed for 2 minutes, scraping bowl occasionally. Stir in enough remaining flour to make a soft dough. Turn out onto a lightly floured board and knead for 8 to 10 minutes or until smooth and elastic. Place in a greased bowl and turn to grease top. Cover and let rise in a warm place, free from draft, for about 1 hour or until doubled in bulk. Punch down and let rise for 30 minutes longer. Punch down and divide into 3 equal pieces. Roll out each piece on a lightly floured board into 8 x 10-inch rectangle and cut into 2-inch squares. Fold each square into a triangle and place 1 inch apart on greased baking sheets. Cover and let rise in a warm place, free from draft, for about 40 minutes or until doubled in bulk. Bake in a 400-degree oven for 10 to 12 minutes or until done. Remove from baking sheets and cool on wire racks. 5 dozen.

KOLACKY

2 3/4 to 3 1/4 c. unsifted flour	**1/3 c. water**
1/4 c. sugar	**2 tbsp. margarine**
1 tsp. salt	**2 eggs, at room temperature**
1 pkg. dry yeast	**Raisin Filling**
1/3 c. milk	

Mix 1 cup flour, sugar, salt and undissolved yeast thoroughly in a large bowl. Combine the milk, water and margarine in a saucepan and place over low heat until liquids are warm. Margarine does not need to melt. Add to dry ingredients gradually and beat for 2 minutes with electric mixer at medium speed, scraping bowl occasionally. Add the eggs and 1/2 cup flour and beat at high speed for 2 minutes, scraping bowl occasionally. Stir in enough remaining flour to make a soft dough. Turn out onto a lightly floured board and knead for 8 to 10 minutes or until smooth and elastic. Place in a greased bowl and turn to grease top. Cover and let rise in a warm place, free from draft, for about 1 hour or until doubled in bulk. Punch down. Turn out onto a lightly floured board and roll out to 1/2-inch thickness. Cut with a 2 1/2-inch biscuit cutter and place circles about 2 inches apart on greased baking sheets. Cover and let rise in warm place, free from draft, for about 1 hour or until doubled in bulk. Press an indentation in the center of each bun, leaving a rim about 1/4 inch wide, and fill with Raisin Filling. Bake in 400-degree oven for about 10 minutes or until done. Remove from baking sheets and cool on wire racks. Sprinkle with confectioners' sugar, if desired.

Raisin Filling

2 c. seedless raisins	**1/2 tsp. ground allspice**
1 c. (firmly packed) light	**1/4 tsp. ground cloves**
brown sugar	**1 1/3 c. water**
3 tbsp. cornstarch	**1/2 c. chopped English walnuts**
1 tsp. ground cinnamon	

Combine all ingredients except the walnuts in a saucepan and bring to a boil, stirring constantly. Cook for 1 minute, then remove from heat. Stir in the walnuts. Cool.

Photograph for this recipe on cover.

ONION ROLLS

3 tbsp. dried onion flakes	**1/4 c. warm water**
1 c. boiling water	**1 pkg. dry yeast**
1/4 c. soft butter	**1 egg**
1 1/2 tsp. salt	**2 tbsp. dried dillweed**
2 tbsp. sugar	**3 c. flour**
1/8 tsp. ginger	

Combine the onion flakes and boiling water. Cover and let stand for 15 minutes. Place the butter, salt and sugar in a bowl. Drain the onion flakes and reserve liquid. Bring reserved liquid to a boil. Pour over butter mixture and stir until dissolved. Cool to lukewarm. Combine the ginger, warm water and yeast and stir until yeast is dissolved. Add to butter mixture and mix well. Beat in the egg, onion and dillweed. Add the flour gradually and beat until well blended. Place in a large greased bowl and turn to grease top. Cover tightly with foil and refrigerate until chilled. Punch down, then fill greased muffin tins 1/3 full. Cover and let rise in a warm place for 30 minutes or until doubled in bulk. Bake at 425 degrees for 12 minutes or until golden.

Evelyn A. Greer, Richwood, West Virginia

BRIOCHES

1 pkg. yeast	1/2 tsp. salt
3 tbsp. warm water	3/4 c. butter or margarine
1 3/4 c. flour	3 eggs, lightly beaten
1 tsp. sugar	

Dissolve the yeast in water. Combine the flour, sugar and salt in a bowl and cut in the butter. Add the eggs and yeast and mix until smooth. Drop by tablespoonfuls into greased and floured custard cups or large muffin cups, placing 3 tablespoonfuls in each, and let rise until doubled in bulk. Bake in 450-degree oven for about 8 minutes. Brush with water and serve warm.

coffee cakes & sweet breads

YEAST

On those very special occasions when you want to delight everyone's palate, your thoughts turn to mouth-watering coffee cakes and sweet breads. It may be a church breakfast meeting, a ladies' get-together, or a school bake sale. But whatever the occasion, the food you send is your representative – and you want it to be your very best. And what could be more impressive than a yeast coffee cake or sweet bread straight from your oven!

The homemakers of *Southern Living* know that sweet yeast breads make a great impression – perhaps that's why this section is so full of their finest, home-tested recipes for these delicacies. Just picture how amazed your family and friends will be when you delight them with Babas with Apricot-Rum Syrup, a fabulously flavored version of a long-time yeast bread favorite. And the coffee cakes you'll discover – Cherry-Pecan Coffee Cake . . . Georgia Peach Coffee Cake . . . Lemon Bread . . . all the great coffee cakes that generations of southern women have been proud to serve.

Every one of these recipes is the tried and proven favorite of a creative homemaker. They are assembled here to help you enhance your culinary reputation – by serving tender-light, still-warm coffee cakes and yeast breads!

PLUM-GOOD COFFEE KUCHEN

3 pkg. dry yeast
1/2 c. warm water
1 tsp. salt
1/2 c. sugar
1/2 c. lukewarm milk
1/3 c. melted butter or
  margarine

4 lge. eggs
1/2 tsp. grated orange peel
1 tsp. vanilla
4 1/2 to 5 c. sifted flour
1 tsp. cream
3 lb. fresh plums, quartered
Streusel Topping

Sprinkle the yeast over warm water in a large bowl and stir until dissolved. Add the salt, sugar, milk and butter and mix. Beat in 3 eggs, orange peel and vanilla. Stir in 3 cups flour and beat with a wooden spoon for 2 minutes. Add enough remaining flour to make a medium-soft dough. Knead on a floured surface for 10 minutes or until smooth and elastic. Place back in bowl. Cover and let rise for 40 minutes or until doubled in bulk. Punch down. Knead on the floured surface just until smooth. Press into bottom and sides of lightly greased 13 x 9 x 2-inch pan. Beat remaining egg with cream and brush on dough. Add the plums, then Streusel Topping. Bake in 350-degree oven for 45 minutes or until browned.

Streusel Topping

1/4 c. butter or margarine
1/3 c. cinnamon sugar
1/2 tsp. vanilla

3/4 c. coarsely chopped walnuts
3/4 c. all-purpose flour

Cream the butter and cinnamon sugar in a bowl. Add remaining ingredients and blend well.

PANETTONE

4 1/2 to 5 1/2 c. unsifted flour	1/2 c. margarine
1/2 c. sugar	4 eggs, at room temperature
1 tsp. salt	1/2 c. chopped citron
2 pkg. dry yeast	1/2 c. seedless raisins
1/2 c. milk	2 tbsp. pine nuts
	1 tbsp. aniseed

Mix 1 1/2 cups flour, sugar, salt and undissolved yeast thoroughly in a large bowl. Combine the milk, 1/2 cup water and margarine in a saucepan and place over low heat until liquids are warm. Margarine does not need to melt. Add to dry ingredients gradually and beat for 2 minutes with electric mixer at medium speed, scraping bowl occasionally. Add 3 eggs and 1/2 cup flour and beat at high speed for 2 minutes, scraping bowl occasionally. Stir in the citron, raisins, pine nuts and aniseed. Add enough remaining flour to make a soft dough. Turn out onto a lightly floured board and knead for 8 to 10 minutes or until smooth and elastic. Place in a greased bowl and turn to grease top. Cover and let rise in a warm place, free from draft, for about 1 hour or until doubled in bulk. Punch down. Cover and let rise again for 30 minutes or until almost doubled in bulk. Punch down. Turn out onto a lightly floured board and divide in half. Form into round balls and place on opposite corners of a greased baking sheet. Cut a cross 1/2 inch deep on top of each ball. Cover and let rise in a warm place, free from draft, for about 1 hour or until doubled in bulk. Beat remaining egg with 1 tablespoon water and brush on loaves. Bake in 350-degree oven for 35 to 45 minutes or until done. Remove from baking sheet and cool on wire racks.

Photograph for this recipe on page 30.

GEORGIA PEACH COFFEE CAKE

2 pkg. dry yeast	5 to 5 1/2 c. flour
1/2 c. warm water	2 tsp. cinnamon
1 1/4 c. sugar	1 c. chopped pecans
3/4 c. butter or margarine	1 c. peach preserves
1/2 c. milk, scalded	1 c. sifted powdered sugar
2 tsp. salt	1 tsp. vanilla
3 eggs	3 tsp. cold milk

Dissolve the yeast in warm water. Combine 1/2 cup sugar, 1/2 cup butter, scalded milk and salt in a bowl and stir until butter is melted. Cool to lukewarm. Blend in eggs and yeast. Add enough flour to form a stiff dough, then knead on a floured surface for 3 to 5 minutes or until smooth. Place in a greased bowl and cover. Let rise in a warm place for 1 hour and 30 minutes. Combine remaining sugar, cinnamon and pecans. Divide the dough in half and roll out each half on a floured board to 20 x 10-inch rectangle. Spread with remaining softened butter. Spread 1/4 cup preserves on each half and sprinkle each half with cinnamon mixture. Roll from 20-inch sides as for jelly roll and seal edges and ends. Form into loops and place on a baking sheet. Cut down center of loops 1/3 of the way through and within 2 inches of ends. Let rise in a warm place for 30 minutes. Spoon 1/4 cup preserves down center of each loop. Bake at 350 degrees for 20 to 25 minutes. Combine remaining ingredients and spread over coffee cakes.

Mrs. James Baker, Tulsa, Oklahoma

CINNAMON TEA RING

Milk	12 1/2 c. flour
5 c. sugar	3 1/2 sticks butter
1 tsp. salt	4 eggs, beaten
1 tsp. mace	4 tbsp. cinnamon
1 tsp. grated lemon rind	3 c. raisins
3 pkg. yeast	3 c. chopped nuts (opt.)
1/2 c. warm water	1 1/2 c. confectioners' sugar

Scald 3 cups milk. Stir in 1 cup sugar, salt, mace and lemon rind and cool to lukewarm. Pour into a bowl. Dissolve yeast in water, then stir into milk mixture. Stir in 6 cups flour and beat until smooth. Let rise until doubled in bulk, then punch down. Cream 1 1/2 sticks butter with 1 cup sugar and stir in the eggs. Stir into milk mixture. Add enough remaining flour to make a soft dough and knead on a floured surface until smooth and elastic. Let rise until doubled in bulk, then punch down. Divide into 6 parts and roll out each part into rectangle about 3/8 inch thick. Combine remaining sugar and cinnamon. Spread each rectangle with 2 tablespoons soft butter, 1/2 cup cinnamon mixture and 1/2 cup each raisins and nuts. Roll each rectangle as for jelly roll and seal edge. Pinch ends together and place on greased cookie sheets. Cut 2/3 of the way through each ring at 1 1/4-inch intervals and turn each cut section on side. Let rise until doubled in bulk. Bake at 350 degrees for 35 minutes. Mix the confectioners' sugar, remaining soft butter and 2 to 3 tablespoons milk. Mixture should be stiff. Spread on rings while hot.

Mrs. John McMath, Birmingham, Alabama

BABAS WITH APRICOT-RUM SYRUP

1/3 c. milk	2 eggs
1 pkg. yeast	1/4 c. seedless raisins
1 c. flour	1 tbsp. rum
1/4 c. sugar	4 tbsp. soft butter
1/8 tsp. salt	

Pour the milk into a saucepan and bring to boiling point. Remove from heat and cool to lukewarm. Add the yeast and stir until dissolved. Let stand for 10 minutes. Place flour in a bowl and add yeast mixture, sugar, salt and eggs. Mix thoroughly. Cover with a towel and let rise in a warm place for 1 hour or until doubled in bulk. Soak the raisins in rum. Add the butter to flour mixture and beat until shiny and no longer sticky. Add raisin mixture and blend well. Place in greased muffin tins, filling 1/2 full. Cover with waxed paper and let rise for about 2 hours or until doubled in bulk. Bake in a 400-degree oven for 12 minutes or until muffins test done. Remove from muffin tins with a fork and place in dessert bowls.

Apricot-Rum Syrup

1 1/2 c. sugar	4 oz. rum
1 1/2 c. apricot nectar	Sweetened whipped cream
2 tsp. lemon juice	

Combine the sugar, apricot nectar, lemon juice and rum in a bowl and stir until sugar is dissolved. Pour over the Babas, turning until the syrup is absorbed. Serve with whipped cream.

Mrs. L. Hyland, Orlando, Florida

APPLE-PRUNE BREAKFAST RING

3/4 c. lukewarm milk	3/4 c. chopped cooked dried
1/4 c. sugar	prunes
1 tsp. salt	1 1/2 c. diced peeled
1 env. dry yeast	Washington golden Delicious
1/4 c. lukewarm water	apples
1 egg, slightly beaten	1 tbsp. lemon juice
1/4 c. soft shortening	1/2 c. (packed) brown sugar
3 1/2 c. (about) sifted flour	1 tsp. cinnamon
2 tbsp. melted butter or	3/4 c. chopped walnuts
margarine	Thin confectioners' sugar icing

Combine the milk, sugar and salt in a bowl. Dissolve the yeast in the water, then stir into the milk mixture. Add the egg and shortening and mix. Stir in just enough flour to make a soft dough. Turn out onto a floured board and knead for about 5 minutes or until smooth and elastic. Place in a greased bowl and turn to grease the surface. Cover and let rise in a warm place for 1 hour and 30 minutes to 2 hours or until doubled in bulk. Punch down, then let rise for 30 to 45 minutes or until doubled in bulk. Roll out on a floured surface to a 9 x 18-inch rectangle and spread with butter. Combine the prunes with remaining ingredients except icing and spread over dough. Roll from long side as for jelly roll and seal edge. Place on a lightly greased baking sheet, seam side down, and form into a circle. Seal ends together. Cut 2/3 of the way into the ring from outer edge at 1-inch intervals with scissors, then turn each section slightly to side. Cover and let rise until doubled in bulk. Bake at 375 degrees for 25 minutes. Frost with the confectioners' sugar icing while warm. 8 servings.

CHERRY-PECAN COFFEE CAKE

1/3 c. sugar	2 eggs, beaten
1/3 c. soft butter	1 c. chopped candied cherries
1/2 tsp. salt	1/2 c. chopped pecans
1/2 c. boiling water	4 1/2 c. sifted flour
Evaporated milk	2/3 c. confectioners' sugar
1 pkg. dry yeast	1/2 tsp. vanilla
1/4 c. warm water	

Combine the sugar, butter and salt in a large mixing bowl. Add the boiling water and stir until butter is melted. Add 3/4 cup evaporated milk. Sprinkle yeast over warm water and stir until dissolved. Add to butter mixture. Stir in the eggs, candied cherries and pecans. Add the flour, 1 cup at a time, beating until smooth after each addition. Cover and let rise in a warm place for 1 hour to 1 hour and 30 minutes or until doubled in bulk. Stir down and beat for 2 minutes. Turn into a well-greased 10-inch tube pan. Cover and let rise for about 45 minutes or until doubled in bulk. Bake in 375-degree oven for 50 to 55 minutes or until browned. Remove from pan and cool on wire rack. Mix the confectioners' sugar, 1 tablespoon evaporated milk and vanilla and spread on the coffee cake. Decorate with candied cherries and pecan halves, if desired.

Mrs. D. R. Garrett, Dallas, Texas

APRICOT BRAID

Unsifted flour	1 1/2 c. dried apricots
6 tbsp. sugar	1 c. boiling water
1 tsp. salt	1 c. (firmly packed) light
1 pkg. yeast	brown sugar
Milk	1/2 tsp. ground cinnamon
4 tbsp. margarine	1 egg yolk, beaten
1 egg, at room temperature	

Mix 3/4 cup flour, 1/4 cup sugar, salt and undissolved yeast thoroughly in a large bowl. Combine 3/4 cup milk and 2 tablespoons margarine in a saucepan and place over low heat until liquid is warm. Margarine does not need to melt. Add to dry ingredients gradually and beat for 2 minutes with electric mixer at medium speed, scraping bowl occasionally. Add egg and 1/4 cup flour and beat at high speed for 2 minutes, scraping bowl occasionally. Stir in enough additional flour to make a soft dough. Turn out onto a lightly floured board and knead for 8 to 10 minutes or until smooth and elastic. Place in a greased bowl and turn to grease top. Cover and let rise in a warm place, free from draft, for 1 hour or until doubled in bulk. Combine the apricots and boiling water in a saucepan and bring to a boil. Reduce heat and simmer, uncovered, for about 25 minutes or until liquid is absorbed and apricots are tender. Press through a sieve. Stir in the brown sugar until dissolved, then cool. Punch dough down. Turn out onto a lightly floured board and divide in half. Roll out each half into a 14 x 8-inch rectangle and place on greased baking sheets. Spread 1/2 of the apricot filling down the center 1/3 of each rectangle. Slit dough at 1-inch intervals along each side of filling, then fold strips at an angle across filling, alternating from side to side. Cover and let rise in a warm place, free from draft, for about 1 hour or until doubled in bulk. Combine 1/3 cup flour, remaining sugar and cinnamon in a bowl and cut in remaining margarine until mixture is crumbly. Mix the egg yolk and 2 tablespoons milk and brush on braids. Sprinkle each braid with half the crumb mixture. Bake in 350-degree oven for about 20 minutes or until done. Remove from baking sheets and cool on wire racks.

Photograph for this recipe on page 2.

FRESH POTATO-FRUIT COFFEE CAKE

1 pkg. dry yeast	2 lge. eggs, lightly beaten
1/2 c. warm water	8 1/2 c. (about) sifted flour
1 c. scalded milk	6 tbsp. melted butter or
1/2 c. shortening	margarine
1 c. fresh hot mashed potatoes	1 c. diced mixed glaceed fruits
Sugar	3/4 tsp. ground cinnamon
2 tsp. salt	1 lge. egg white

Sprinkle the yeast over warm water and stir until dissolved. Mix the milk, shortening, potatoes, 1/3 cup sugar and salt in a large bowl and cool to lukewarm. Add yeast and eggs and blend well. Add 1 1/2 cups flour and mix well. Cover and let rise in a warm place for about 1 hour or until bubbly. Stir in enough remaining flour to make a stiff dough. Turn onto a lightly floured board and knead until smooth and elastic. Place in a lightly greased bowl and turn to grease surface. Cover and refrigerate overnight. Roll out on a lightly floured board to 1-inch thickness. Cut with a 2-inch biscuit cutter. Dip each round into melted butter, then in glaceed fruits. Combine 3/4 cup sugar and cinnamon and dip rounds in the cinnamon mixture. Stand up in 2 greased and lightly floured 8-inch ring molds. Sprinkle with any remaining fruits. Beat the egg white until foamy and brush on cakes. Let rise in a warm place for about 1 hour or until doubled in bulk. Bake in a 350-degree oven for 35 minutes. Serve warm.

Photograph for this recipe on page 14.

PULL-APART

1 1/2 c. sugar	1/2 c. sour cream
1 c. butter	4 c. flour
1 tsp. vanilla	3 egg whites
3 eggs	1 c. chopped nuts
1 pkg. dry yeast	2 tsp. cinnamon
1/2 c. lukewarm milk	

Cream 1/2 cup sugar, butter and vanilla in a bowl, then stir in the eggs. Dissolve the yeast in lukewarm milk and stir into creamed mixture. Add the sour cream and flour alternately, then refrigerate overnight. Remove from refrigerator and leave at room temperature for 1 hour. Roll out on a floured surface to 1/8-inch thick rectangle. Beat egg whites in a bowl until soft peaks form, then beat until stiff, adding 1/2 cup sugar gradually. Spread over dough. Sprinkle with nuts, cinnamon and remaining sugar. Roll as for jelly roll and cut crosswise into 6 pieces. Place, cut side up, in a large, greased tube pan and let rise for 2 hours. Bake at 350 degrees for 30 to 40 minutes or until browned.

Geraldine Pace, St. Augustine, Florida

LEMON BREAD

1 pkg. yeast	2 eggs, beaten
1/4 c. warm water	1/2 c. melted butter
1/2 c. milk	2 tbsp. fine bread crumbs
1/2 c. sugar	16 whole blanched almonds
1/2 tsp. salt	1/2 c. raisins
2 1/2 c. sifted flour	1 tsp. grated lemon rind

Dissolve the yeast in warm water. Combine the milk, sugar, salt and 1 1/2 cups flour in a bowl and mix well. Stir in the yeast mixture and beat until smooth. Add the eggs and beat well. Stir in butter, 1 tablespoon at a time. Add remaining flour and beat for 5 minutes. Cover and let rise in a warm place for about 1 hour and 30 minutes or until doubled in bulk. Grease a loaf pan and sprinkle with crumbs. Arrange whole almonds in bottom. Stir down dough and mix in raisins and lemon rind. Spoon into prepared pan and let rise for about 1 hour and 15 minutes or until doubled in bulk. Bake at 350 degrees for 40 to 50 minutes. Ground almonds may be substituted for bread crumbs.

Terry Haga, Warstington County, Virginia

COFFEE BREAKERS

4 1/2 to 5 1/2 c. unsifted flour	3/4 c. margarine
1/2 c. sugar	2 eggs, at room temperature
1 1/2 tsp. salt	Light brown sugar
2 pkg. dry yeast	2 tsp. light corn syrup
1/2 c. milk	3/4 c. chopped pecans
1/2 c. water	Melted margarine
	2 tsp. ground cinnamon

Mix 1 2/3 cups flour, sugar, salt and undissolved yeast thoroughly in a large bowl. Combine the milk, water and 1/4 cup margarine in a saucepan and place over low heat until liquids are warm. Margarine does not need to melt. Add to dry ingredients gradually and beat for 2 minutes with electric mixer at medium speed, scraping bowl occasionally. Add eggs and 1/2 cup flour and beat at high speed for 2 minutes, scraping bowl occasionally. Stir in enough remaining flour to make a soft dough. Turn out onto a lightly floured board and knead for 8 to 10 minutes or until smooth and elastic. Place in a greased bowl and turn to grease top. Cover and let rise in a warm place, free from draft, for about 1 hour or until doubled in bulk. Melt remaining margarine in a saucepan. Add 2/3 cup firmly packed brown sugar and corn syrup and bring to a rolling boil. Pour into two 15 1/2 x 10 1/2 x 1-inch jelly roll pans immediately and sprinkle with pecans. Punch dough down. Turn out onto a lightly floured board and divide in half. Roll half the dough into a 12-inch square and brush with melted margarine. Combine 1/2 cup firmly packed brown sugar and cinnamon. Sprinkle center 1/3 of the dough with 1/4 of the cinnamon mixture and fold 1/3 of the dough over center third. Sprinkle with 1/4 the cinnamon mixture. Fold remaining 1/3 of the dough over to make a 12-inch strip. Cut into twelve 1-inch pieces. Hold ends of each piece and twist 2 or 3 times in opposite direction. Seal ends firmly. Place about 1 1/2 inches apart in prepared pan. Repeat with remaining dough and filling. Cover and let rise in a warm place, free from draft, for about 1 hour or until doubled in bulk. Bake in 400-degree oven for 15 to 20 minutes or until done. Invert rolls onto plates or wire racks to cool. Serve warm. 24 rolls.

Photograph for this recipe on page 25.

HONEY-ALMOND BRAID

1 pkg. yeast	1 1/2 tsp. grated orange rind
1/4 c. warm water	3 c. sifted all-purpose flour
1/2 c. scalded milk	1 c. blanched ground almonds
1 tsp. salt	1 1/4 c. honey
1/2 tsp. ground cardamom	3/4 c. melted butter or
1/4 c. sugar	margarine
1/3 c. shortening	1/4 c. blanched toasted whole
1 egg, slightly beaten	almonds

Dissolve the yeast in the water. Mix the milk, salt, cardamom, sugar and shortening in a large mixing bowl until sugar is dissolved and shortening melted. Cool to lukewarm. Add the egg and orange rind and mix well. Stir in 1 1/2 cups flour, then yeast. Add remaining flour and beat well. Scrape from sides of bowl and cover with a damp cloth. Let rise in a warm place for about 1 hour and 30 minutes or until doubled in bulk. Punch down and let rest for 10 minutes. Divide into 3 parts. Roll out each part on a floured surface to a 16 x 5-inch rectangle. Mix the ground almonds, 3/4 cup honey and 1/2 cup butter for filling. Spread 1/3 of the filling on each rectangle and roll from long side as for jelly roll. Seal edge and ends. Place on a greased baking sheet and braid, tucking ends under firmly. Cover and let rise for about 30 minutes or until light. Bake at 400 degrees for 20 to 25 minutes. Split the whole almonds in halves and mix with remaining honey and butter. Spread over the braid. Serve warm or cold.

FROSTED ORANGE ROLLS

1 pkg. dry yeast	2 tbsp. melted butter
1/4 c. lukewarm water	1 tbsp. grated orange peel
1 egg	3/4 c. orange juice
2 tbsp. sugar	3 c. sifted flour
1 1/2 tsp. salt	1 diced orange, sweetened

Dissolve the yeast in water. Beat the egg in a mixing bowl. Add yeast, sugar, salt, butter, orange peel, orange juice and enough flour to make a soft dough and beat until smooth. Turn out on a floured board and knead until smooth and elastic. Place in a greased bowl and turn to grease top. Place bowl in pan of warm water and let rise for about 1 hour or until doubled in bulk. Punch down and let stand for several minutes. Roll out about 1/2 inch thick on a floured board and cut with biscuit cutter. Let stand on board for 10 to 15 minutes, then crease each circle with back of a knife. Brush with additional melted butter and place piece of orange on circle. Fold over and press lightly. Place on greased baking sheets. Cover with damp cloth and let rise until doubled in bulk. Bake in 425-degree oven for 15 to 20 minutes. 3 dozen.

Orange-Butter Icing

1 tsp. grated orange peel	1 tbsp. lemon juice
1 tbsp. soft butter	3 tbsp. (about) orange juice
1 c. sifted powdered sugar	

Mix the orange peel and butter in a bowl. Add powdered sugar alternately with juices, beating well after each addition. Spread on warm rolls.

Mrs. Charles Winters. Biloxi, Mississippi

PRALINE ROLLS

1 pkg. dry yeast	2/3 c. butter
1/4 c. warm water	1/3 c. scalded milk
2 1/4 c. sifted flour	1 egg
2 tbsp. sugar	3/4 c. (packed) brown sugar
2 tsp. baking powder	1/2 c. chopped nuts
1/2 tsp. salt	

Dissolve the yeast in warm water. Sift the flour, sugar, baking powder and salt together into a mixing bowl and cut in 1/3 cup butter until mixture resembles fine crumbs. Cool the milk to lukewarm, then stir into flour mixture. Stir in the egg and yeast and beat well. Place on a floured surface and roll out to 15 x 10-inch rectangle. Cream remaining butter and brown sugar until fluffy and spread half the mixture over dough. Sprinkle with nuts and roll as for jelly roll. Cut into 1-inch slices and place on greased cookie sheets. Spread with remaining sugar mixture. Let rise in a warm place for about 45 minutes or until doubled in bulk. Bake at 425 degrees for 10 to 12 minutes.

Emma Falkenberry, Columbia, South Carolina

BAKED ALMOND DOUGHNUTS

3/4 c. scalded milk	3/4 tsp. nutmeg
6 tbsp. salad oil	4 1/4 to 4 1/2 c. sifted flour
1/3 c. sugar	1 to 1 1/4 c. chopped roasted
1 1/2 tsp. salt	almonds
2 pkg. yeast	1/2 c. melted butter or
1/4 c. warm water	margarine
2 eggs, beaten	Glaze

Mix the milk with oil, sugar and salt and cool to lukewarm. Dissolve the yeast in warm water in a large bowl, then stir in the milk mixture, eggs and nutmeg. Blend in the flour and 1/2 cup almonds gradually. Turn out on a floured board and knead until smooth and elastic. Return to bowl and grease top of dough. Cover and let rise in a warm place until doubled in bulk. Turn out on a floured board and roll to 1/2-inch thickness. Cut into 2 1/4-inch rounds with a doughnut cutter. Place 2 inches apart on greased baking sheets and brush with 1/4 cup butter. Let rise in a warm place for 20 to 30 minutes. Bake at 425 degrees for 8 to 10 minutes. Brush with remaining butter, then cool enough to handle. Dip in warm Glaze, then in remaining almonds. Let stand to set Glaze. 1 1/2-2 dozen.

Glaze

1/4 c. corn syrup	1 6-oz. package chocolate or
3 tbsp. water	butterscotch pieces
2 tbsp. salad oil	

Combine the corn syrup, water and oil in a saucepan. Bring to a boil, then remove from heat. Add the chocolate pieces and stir until chocolate is melted.

DELICIOUS CRULLERS

2 pkg. dry yeast	1 1/2 tsp. salt
1/2 c. warm water	1/4 c. shortening
1/2 c. milk, scalded	3 1/4 to 3 3/4 c. sifted flour
1/3 c. sugar	1 egg, slightly beaten

Dissolve the yeast in water. Mix the milk, sugar, salt and shortening in a bowl until shortening is melted and cool to lukewarm. Add 1 cup flour and beat well. Add the egg and yeast. Add enough remaining flour to make a soft dough and mix well. Knead on a lightly floured surface for about 8 minutes. Place in greased bowl and turn to grease the surface. Cover and let rise for about 1 hour and 30 minutes or until doubled in bulk. Punch down and let rise until doubled in bulk. Punch down and let rest for 10 minutes. Roll out on a lightly floured surface into 12 x 9-inch rectangle. Cut in half crosswise and cut each half into 12 strips. Roll each strip to make a 10-inch strip and twist. Cover and let rise for about 45 minutes or until almost doubled in bulk. Fry in deep fat at 375 degrees for about 2 minutes, turning once, then drain. Brush with confectioners' icing, if desired. 2 dozen.

Frances Irving, Raleigh, North Carolina

FILLED DOUGHNUTS

2 pkg. dry yeast	1 tsp. salt
1/2 c. warm water	2 eggs
3/4 c. milk, scalded	4 1/2 to 5 c. sifted flour
1/3 c. shortening	18 prunes
1/2 c. sugar	

Dissolve the yeast in water. Combine the milk, shortening, 1/4 cup sugar and salt in a bowl and stir until shortening is dissolved. Cool to lukewarm. Add the yeast, eggs and 2 cups flour and beat well. Add enough remaining flour to make a soft dough. Turn out on a lightly floured surface and knead for about 8 minutes or until smooth and elastic. Place in a greased bowl and turn to grease surface. Cover and let rise for about 50 minutes or until doubled in bulk. Cook the prunes according to package directions, adding remaining sugar to water before cooking. Drain and cool. Halve and remove pits. Cut dough in half and roll out 3/8 inch thick on a floured surface. Cut with a 2 1/2-inch biscuit cutter. Place a prune half on each round and fold dough over prune. Seal edges. Cover and let rise in a warm place for 20 minutes or until doubled in bulk. Fry in deep fat at 375 degrees for about 1 minute on each side or until golden brown. Drain on paper towels and roll in additional sugar. 3 dozen.

Dorothy Pfieffer, Atlanta, Georgia

YEAST DOUGHNUTS

1/2 c. milk, scalded	1/2 c. warm water
1/2 c. sugar	2 eggs
1 tsp. salt	4 c. sifted all-purpose flour
1/2 c. soft butter or margarine	3/4 tsp. nutmeg
2 pkg. dry yeast	Salad oil or shortening

Mix the milk, sugar, salt and butter in a bowl and stir until butter is melted. Cool to lukewarm. Dissolve the yeast in warm water, then stir into milk mixture. Add the eggs, 2 cups flour and nutmeg and beat until smooth. Stir in remaining flour and beat until smooth. Cover with a towel and let rise in a warm place, free from drafts, for about 1 hour or until doubled in bulk. Punch down. Turn out onto a well-floured pastry cloth and knead 10 times until dough is smooth. Cover with a bowl and let rest for 10 minutes. Roll out 1/2 inch thick and cut with a floured doughnut cutter. Heat 1 1/2 to 2 inches of salad oil in an electric skillet or heavy saucepan to 375 degrees. Fry doughnuts in oil until golden brown on both sides. Drain on paper towels and cool or wire racks. 20 doughnuts.

Mrs. Richard E. Adams, Tucson, Arizona

GLAZED DOUGHNUTS

2 pkg. dry yeast	7 1/2 c. flour
1/2 c. warm water	1 tsp. nutmeg (opt.)
1 c. boiling water	Salad oil or shortening
1/4 c. shortening	3 c. unsifted confectioners'
3/4 c. sugar	sugar
1 1/3 c. milk	1 tsp. vanilla
2 lge. eggs	

Dissolve the yeast in warm water. Combine the boiling water, shortening and sugar in a large bowl and stir in 1 cup milk. Add eggs and yeast. Add the flour and nutmeg and mix until smooth. Place in a greased bowl and cover. Chill for 2 to 3 hours or overnight. Divide in half and roll out on a floured board to 1/2-inch thickness. Cut with 3-inch doughnut cutter and let rise in a warm place until doubled in bulk. Fry in at least 2 inches of oil at 375 degrees until lightly browned, then drain on absorbent paper. Combine the confectioners' sugar, remaining milk and vanilla and beat until smooth. Spread over doughnuts while warm. May coat with confectioners' sugar or sugar instead of glaze, if desired. 4 1/2 dozen.

Anne Johnson, Tulsa, Oklahoma

RAISED DOUGHNUTS

1 c. milk, scalded	2 tbsp. lukewarm water
2/3 c. sugar	5 c. (about) flour
3 tbsp. shortening	2 eggs, well beaten
1 tsp. salt	1 tsp. nutmeg
1 pkg. dry yeast	Powdered sugar

Mix the milk, sugar, shortening and salt in a bowl and cool to lukewarm. Dissolve yeast in water, then stir into milk mixture. Add 2 cups flour and mix well. Let rise in a warm place until light. Add the eggs, nutmeg and enough remaining flour to make a soft dough. Cover and let rise until doubled in bulk. Knead on a floured surface until smooth. Roll out 1/2 inch thick and cut with a doughnut cutter. Cover and let rise in warm place until doubled in bulk. Fry in deep fat at 370 degrees until puffy and brown. Turn and fry on other side. Drain on absorbent paper and sprinkle with powdered sugar while warm. 30 doughnuts.

Mrs. Elsie S. Trader, Benson, North Carolina

corn breads & casserole breads

YEAST

Few foods are quite so southern as corn breads. There are almost as many variations on this theme as there are creative southern homemakers who prepare corn breads — and in the section that follows, you'll find the best recipes for corn breads which use yeast in their preparation. Featured with these are casserole breads, those easy-to-prepare, attractive breads you bake in various-shaped casserole dishes.

Introduce your family and friends to the diversity of corn breads — serve Cornmeal-Raisin Bread at breakfast brunch . . . Deep South Corn Pones with your next roast or ham . . . and Sourdough Corn Bread when a meal needs that certain something to pep it up. Then you'll discover why southern homemakers depend upon corn bread.

Discover how you can bring a variety of shapes and flavors to your family's table with casserole breads. There are recipes here for Pumpernickel Bread . . . dark, rich, and loved by generations of southern families, for Anise Bread, Casserole Onion Bread, Cheese Casserole Bread, and Whole Wheat Batter Bread.

These are just a few of the family-approved recipes you'll find in this section, recipes you'll depend upon to introduce variety and delicious flavors to your every meal!

45

SOURDOUGH CORN BREAD

1 c. Sourdough Starter	2 tbsp. sugar
1 1/2 c. yellow cornmeal	1/4 c. melted margarine
1 1/2 c. evaporated milk	1/2 tsp. salt
2 eggs, beaten	3/4 tsp. soda

Mix the Sourdough Starter, cornmeal, milk, eggs and sugar in a large bowl and stir in the margarine, salt and soda. Pour into a 10-inch greased frying pan. Bake at 425 degrees for 25 to 30 minutes. Serve hot.

Sourdough Starter

1 c. milk	1 c. flour

Pour the milk into a glass jar or crock and let stand at room temperature for 24 hours. Stir in the flour and cover with cheesecloth. Place outdoors for several hours. Leave uncovered indoors for 2 to 5 days or until bubbling. Store in refrigerator.

Mrs. Paul Yancy, Jr., Fort Sumner, New Mexico

CORNMEAL-RAISIN BREAD

2 pkg. dry yeast	1/3 c. shortening
1/2 c. warm water	2 eggs, beaten
1 1/3 c. milk, scalded	1 1/2 c. cornmeal
3/4 c. sugar	6 c. all-purpose flour
1 tbsp. salt	1 1/2 c. raisins

Dissolve the yeast in warm water. Pour the milk over sugar, salt and shortening in a bowl and stir until shortening is melted. Cool to lukewarm. Stir in the eggs and cornmeal. Add yeast and 3 cups flour and beat until smooth. Stir in remaining flour and raisins and beat until blended. Cover and let rise in a warm place for about 1 hour or until doubled in bulk. Stir down and beat vigorously, for about 30 seconds. Place in 2 greased loaf pans. Cover and let rise in a warm place for 45 minutes or until almost doubled in bulk. Bake in 375-degree oven for 45 to 50 minutes. Remove from pans and cool.

Mrs. Gustava Murks, Florence, Alabama

DEEP SOUTH CORN PONES

1/2 c. yellow cornmeal	2 tbsp. margarine
2 tbsp. salt	2 pkg. yeast
1/2 c. molasses	5 1/2 c. (about) unsifted flour

Pour 1 1/2 cups water into a saucepan and bring to a boil. Stir in cornmeal slowly. Add the salt, molasses and margarine and stir until smooth. Pour into a large bowl and cool to lukewarm. Dissolve the yeast in 1/2 cup warm water, then stir into cornmeal mixture. Add half the flour and beat until smooth. Add enough remaining flour to make a soft dough and mix well. Turn onto lightly floured board and knead for about 8 minutes or until smooth and elastic. Place in a greased bowl and turn to grease top. Cover and let rise in a warm place, free from draft for about 1 hour or until doubled in bulk. Punch down. Turn onto a lightly floured board and divide into 15 parts. Shape into small loaves and place in small greased loaf pans. Cover and let rise in a warm place, free from draft, until doubled in bulk. Bake in 375-degree oven for about 20 minutes or until done.

Mrs. R. N. Fourr, Elfrida, Arizona

SESAME-RAISED CORNMEAL MUFFINS

1 pkg. dry yeast	1/2 c. butter or margarine
1/4 c. warm water	2 c. scalded milk
1 c. cornmeal	4 c. sifted flour
1/2 c. sugar	2 eggs, beaten
1 tbsp. salt	Sesame seed

Dissolve the yeast in the water. Place the cornmeal, sugar, salt and butter in a bowl. Add the milk and stir occasionally until the butter melts. Cool to luke-warm. Beat in 1 cup flour and eggs, then the yeast. Beat in remaining flour. Mixture will be very stiff. Cover and let rise in a warm place for about 1 hour or until doubled in bulk. Stir down and fill 24 greased medium muffin cups 3/4 full. Cover and let rise in a warm place for about 45 minutes or until nearly doubled in bulk. Sprinkle with sesame seed. Bake in a 400-degree oven for about 15 minutes or until golden brown. Serve hot.

COLOSSAL CORN BREAD

1 pkg. dry yeast	1 tbsp. salt
1/4 c. warm water	7 c. sifted flour
2 c. milk, scalded	2 eggs, well beaten
1/3 c. sugar	1 c. yellow cornmeal
1/3 c. shortening	

Dissolve the yeast in warm water. Combine the milk, sugar, shortening and salt in a bowl and stir in 3 cups flour. Add the eggs, yeast and cornmeal and stir. Add remaining flour and mix well. Knead on a floured surface for about 10 minutes or until smooth. Place in a greased bowl and let rise in a warm place until doubled in bulk. Place in 2 loaf pans and let rise for about 20 minutes. Bake at 375 degrees for 35 minutes.

Mrs. Harold Pitts, Nashville, Tennessee

RAISED CORN BREAD

1 c. buttermilk, scalded	1 1/2 tsp. salt
3 tbsp. sugar	1/4 c. instant nonfat dry milk
2 pkg. dry yeast	1/2 c. wheat germ
1 c. cornmeal	2 eggs, beaten
1/2 c. whole wheat flour	3 tbsp. bacon drippings

Mix the buttermilk and sugar and cool to lukewarm. Add the yeast and stir until dissolved. Sift cornmeal, whole wheat flour, salt and milk together and stir in wheat germ. Add eggs and drippings to milk mixture and mix well. Stir in the cornmeal mixture. Pour into a greased 8 x 8 x 2-inch baking pan. Bake in 350-degree oven for 30 minutes.

Mrs. Afton Hurley, Randleman, North Carolina

DELICIOUS YEAST CORN BREAD

1 egg, beaten	2 tbsp. sugar
1/4 c. melted shortening	1 tsp. salt
1 c. buttermilk	1 pkg. yeast
1 c. cornmeal	1/4 c. warm water
1/4 tsp. soda	1 1/2 c. (about) sifted flour

Mix the egg, shortening, buttermilk, cornmeal, soda, sugar and salt in a bowl. Dissolve the yeast in warm water. Stir into cornmeal mixture and beat until light and fluffy. Add enough flour to make a soft dough and mix well. Place on floured surface and knead until smooth and elastic. Place in a greased bowl and turn to grease top. Cover with a cloth and let rise until doubled in bulk. Punch down and place in a greased loaf pan. Bake in 350-degree oven for 50 minutes to 1 hour. Remove from pan and wet top with cold water. Place on side and cover with a cloth. Cool.

Mrs. Florence A. DeHerich, Columbia, Tennessee

CORNMEAL BREAD

2 pkg. dry yeast	1 tsp. salt
1 c. warm water	1 egg, well beaten
1/4 c. sugar	2 c. white cornmeal
1/2 c. shortening	Flour

Dissolve the yeast in warm water in a bowl. Add the sugar and shortening and let stand until bubbly. Add the salt and egg. Add the cornmeal and enough flour to make a stiff dough and mix well. Knead on a floured board for about 5 minutes. Place in a bowl and let rise until doubled in bulk. Punch down and let stand for 10 minutes. Shape into 2 loaves and place in greased loaf pans. Let rise until doubled in bulk. Bake in 400-degree oven for 20 minutes. Reduce temperature to 350 degrees and bake for 25 minutes longer. Let stand for 24 hours before slicing.

Mrs. J. W. Eisenhauer, Siloam Springs, Arkansas

RAISED CORNMEAL GRIDDLE CAKES

1 pkg. yeast	1 1/3 c. cornmeal
1/2 c. lukewarm water	4 tsp. sugar
2 1/2 c. scalded milk	1 tsp. salt
2 2/3 c. sifted flour	2 eggs, well beaten

Dissolve the yeast in lukewarm water. Cool the milk in a bowl until lukewarm. Add the yeast and mix well. Mix dry ingredients and stir into yeast mixture. Cover and let stand overnight in a warm place. Add eggs and mix well. Let stand for 10 to 15 minutes. Drop from spoon onto hot greased griddle and cook until brown. Turn and brown on other side. 3 dozen.

Mrs. Leon Dollins, Elmer, Oklahoma

YEAST CORN BREAD

1 1/4 c. cornmeal	1 tbsp. salt
4 c. boiling water	1 pkg. yeast
1 c. molasses	1/4 c. warm water
2 tbsp. sugar	Flour
1 tbsp. lard	

Stir the cornmeal into boiling water in a saucepan and cook, stirring, for several minutes or until consistency of mush. Remove from heat. Add the molasses, sugar, lard and salt and cool. Dissolve the yeast in warm water, then stir into cornmeal mixture. Add enough flour to make a stiff dough. Knead on a floured board for 20 minutes. Place in a bowl and let rise overnight. Shape into 2 loaves and place in 2 greased loaf pans. Let rise until doubled in bulk. Bake at 350 degrees for about 45 minutes or until done.

Mrs. Laura Richardson, Marmaduke, Arkansas

GRAND NATIONAL BREAD

1/2 c. scalded milk	1 1/2 tsp. salt
1 pkg. yeast	1 egg
1/4 c. warm water	1 1/2 c. minced cooked ham
1 c. mashed potatoes	(opt.)
1/4 c. cooking oil	4 to 4 1/2 c. all-purpose flour
2 tbsp. sugar	1/4 c. sesame seed

Cool the milk to lukewarm. Dissolve the yeast in the water in a large mixing bowl, then stir in the milk, potatoes, oil, sugar and salt. Add the egg, ham and 2 cups flour and beat well. Cover and let rise in a warm place for 1 hour to 1 hour and 30 minutes or until doubled in bulk. Stir in enough remaining flour to form a stiff dough. Knead on a floured surface for 3 to 5 minutes or until smooth. Sprinkle 1 tablespoon sesame seed on a greased cookie sheet. Roll out half the dough on sheet to a 14 x 10-inch rectangle. Brush with additional milk and sprinkle with 1 tablespoon sesame seed. Repeat with remaining dough and sesame seed. Cover and let rise for about 1 hour or until light. Bake at 400 degrees for 15 to 20 minutes or until golden brown. Cool and cut into 1-inch squares. May use bread for dipping into Swiss cheese fondue. 8-10 servings.

Photograph for this recipe on page 44.

ANISE BREAD

2 pkg. dry yeast	2 tsp. salt
2 c. warm water	2 tbsp. honey
2 c. whole wheat flour	3 tbsp. soft margarine
3 c. flour	2 tsp. crushed aniseed

Dissolve the yeast in water in a mixing bowl. Mix the whole wheat flour and flour. Add the salt, honey, margarine and half the flour mixture to the yeast mixture and mix well. Add remaining flour mixture and mix well. Cover and let rise in a warm place for about 1 hour or until doubled in bulk. Sprinkle 1 teaspoon aniseed on bottom and sides of a greased 2-quart casserole. Stir remaining aniseed into dough, then place in the casserole. Bake at 350 degrees for about 1 hour.

Mrs. Florence Harris, Charleston, South Carolina

BANANA BREAD

2 pkg. dry yeast	2 tbsp. sugar
1 c. warm water	3 tbsp. melted shortening
6 c. rye flour	3 c. mashed ripe bananas
1 tbsp. salt	

Dissolve the yeast in warm water in a large mixing bowl. Mix half the flour and remaining ingredients. Add to the yeast water and mix well. Add remaining flour gradually and mix until smooth. Turn out onto a floured surface and knead for 10 minutes. Place in a greased bowl and turn to grease surface. Cover and let rise in a warm place until doubled in bulk. Turn out on a floured surface and knead for 3 minutes. Mold into loaves and place in 2 greased casseroles. Cover with a damp cloth and let rise until doubled in bulk. Bake in 425-degree oven for 12 minutes. Reduce temperature to 350 degrees and bake for 45 minutes longer. Remove bread to racks and cool.

Mrs. Bertha Miller, Richmond, Virginia

CASSEROLE ONION BREAD

1 c. milk, scalded	1 tsp. onion salt
3 tbsp. sugar	1/2 tsp. celery salt
2 tsp. salt	2 tbsp. margarine or butter
1 1/2 tbsp. shortening	3/4 c. chopped onion
2 pkg. yeast	1 egg yolk
1 c. warm water	1 tsp. cold water
4 1/2 c. sifted flour	

Mix the milk, sugar, salt and shortening in a bowl and cool to lukewarm. Dissolve the yeast in the warm water, then stir into milk mixture. Mix the flour, onion salt and celery salt. Add to yeast mixture and stir until well blended. Cover with a towel and let rise in a warm place for about 40 minutes or until tripled in bulk. Stir down, then beat vigorously for about 30 seconds. Turn into a greased 2-quart casserole. Bake at 375 degrees for 40 minutes. Melt the butter in a saucepan over low heat. Add the onion and cover. Cook for about 5 minutes, then cool. Beat egg yolk until light. Add cold water and mix well. Combine with onion and spoon over bread. Bake for 20 minutes longer. Remove from casserole and cool on a rack.

Mrs. Warren P. Carson, Savannah, Georgia

CORNMEAL BREAD

12 slices lean bacon	1 c. boiling water
2 pkg. dry yeast	6 c. flour
2 c. warm water	2 tbsp. sugar
2 tsp. salt	1/4 c. chopped green pepper
1 c. yellow cornmeal	2 tbsp. chopped pimento

Fry the bacon in a skillet until crisp, then drain on paper towels. Crumble the bacon. Reserve bacon drippings. Dissolve the yeast in warm water. Mix the salt, reserved drippings and 1/2 cup cornmeal in a bowl. Add the boiling water and mix well. Cool to lukewarm. Add the yeast mixture and stir well. Add half the flour and beat until smooth. Stir in the bacon, remaining cornmeal, flour and remaining ingredients. Cover and let rise in warm place until doubled in bulk. Sprinkle sides and bottom of a greased 2-quart casserole with additional cornmeal. Stir down dough and beat for 30 seconds. Spoon into the casserole and sprinkle with additional cornmeal. Bake in a 350-degree oven for 1 hour or until brown. Cool on a rack.

Vera Alford, Miami, Florida

RAISIN BREAD

2 pkg. yeast
1/4 c. melted butter or
   margarine
2 1/2 c. lukewarm milk
1 1/4 c. water

1/4 c. molasses or corn syrup
1 tsp. salt
5 3/4 c. graham flour
5 3/4 c. flour
1 c. raisins

Place the yeast in a large bowl. Mix the margarine, milk, water and molasses. Pour over the yeast and stir until dissolved. Add the salt, flours and raisins and mix thoroughly. Place in 2 round greased casseroles and let rise until doubled in bulk. Bake in 350-degree oven for about 1 hour or until bread tests done. Wrap each loaf in a towel and cool.

Photograph for this recipe on page 1.

CASSEROLE CHEESE BREAD

1 c. milk, scalded
3 tbsp. sugar
1 tbsp. salt
1 tbsp. butter or margarine

2 pkg. dry yeast
1 c. warm water
1 c. grated Cheddar cheese
4 1/2 c. flour

Mix the milk, sugar, salt and butter in a bowl and cool to lukewarm. Dissolve the yeast in the warm water, then stir into milk mixture. Add the cheese and flour and stir until well blended. Cover and let rise in a warm place for about 45 minutes or until doubled in bulk. Stir down. Beat for about 30 seconds and turn into a greased 1 1/2-quart casserole. Bake at 375 degrees for about 1 hour.

Mrs. Jerry Little, Weiner, Arkansas

HERB BREAD

2 pkg. dry yeast
2 c. warm water
2 tbsp. melted butter or
   margarine

2 tsp. salt
2 tbsp. sugar
1 tbsp. dried rosemary leaves
6 c. all-purpose flour

Dissolve the yeast in warm water in a large bowl, then stir in the butter. Blend remaining ingredients and stir into the yeast mixture. Beat with electric mixer at medium speed for about 2 minutes or until smooth. Scrape down side of bowl and cover with a cloth. Let rise until doubled in bulk. Stir down and turn into a greased 2-quart casserole. Bake in 375-degree oven for about 1 hour. Cool on a rack.

Mrs. Harold Thompson, Dothan, Alabama

HERB BATTER BREAD

1 pkg. dry yeast
1 1/4 c. warm water
2 tbsp. soft shortening
2 tsp. salt
2 tbsp. sugar

3 c. sifted flour
1/2 tsp. nutmeg
1 tsp. sage
2 tsp. caraway seed
Melted butter

Dissolve the yeast in warm water in a mixing bowl. Add the shortening, salt, sugar and half the flour and beat for 2 minutes, scraping side and bottom of bowl frequently. Add remaining flour, nutmeg, sage and caraway seed and blend until smooth. Cover with a cloth and let rise in a warm place for about 30 minutes or until doubled in bulk. Beat about 25 strokes and spread in a greased casserole. Let rise for about 40 minutes or until doubled in bulk. Bake at 375 degrees for 45 to 50 minutes or until brown. Remove from casserole onto rack and brush top of bread with butter.

Mrs. M. D. Hickman, Fort Polk, Louisiana

INDIVIDUAL CASSEROLE LOAVES

1/2 c. warm water	2 1-lb. cans pear halves,
1 pkg. yeast	drained
2 1/4 c. unsifted flour	1/4 c. (firmly packed) dark
1/2 c. melted	brown sugar
margarine	1/4 c. margarine
3 eggs, beaten	1/2 tsp. cinnamon
1/4 c. sugar	1/2 tsp. nutmeg
1/2 tsp. salt	Whipped cream (opt.)

Pour the warm water into a large, warm bowl. Sprinkle with yeast and stir until dissolved. Stir in 1/2 cup flour. Cover and let rise in a warm place, free from draft, for about 30 minutes. Blend in 1 1/2 cups flour, melted margarine, eggs, sugar and salt and beat until well blended. Cover and let rise in a warm place, free from draft, for about 1 hour or until doubled in bulk. Stir down. Cover and refrigerate for at least 2 hours. Press into 12 greased individual casseroles, bringing dough about 1 inch up the side of each casserole. Place a pear half, cut side up, in each casserole. Combine remaining flour, brown sugar, margarine, cinnamon and nutmeg and sprinkle over pears. Let rise, free from draft, for 30 minutes. Bake in 375-degree oven for about 15 minutes or until done. Serve warm topped with whipped cream.

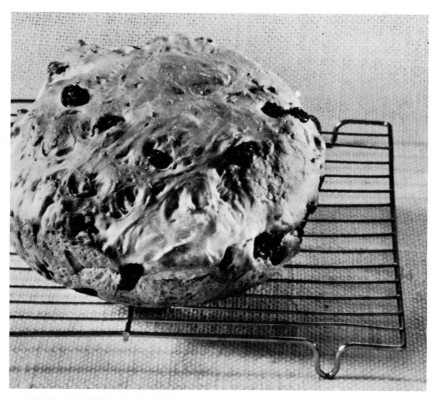

RAISIN CASSEROLE BREAD

1 c. scalded milk	2 pkg. yeast
1/2 c. sugar	1 egg, beaten
1 tsp. salt	4 1/2 c. (about) unsifted flour
1/4 c. margarine	1 c. seedless raisins
1/2 c. warm water	

Mix the milk, sugar, salt and margarine and cool to lukewarm. Pour the water into a large, warm bowl. Add the yeast and stir until dissolved. Stir in the milk mixture, egg and 3 cups flour and beat until smooth. Stir in enough remaining flour to make a stiff dough. Cover and let rise in a warm place, free from draft, for about 1 hour or until doubled in bulk. Stir down. Stir in the raisins and turn into 2 greased 1-quart casseroles. Bake in 350-degree oven for 40 to 45 minutes or until done.

GARLIC CASSEROLE BREAD

1 c. milk, scalded	2 pkg. yeast
3 tbsp. sugar	1 c. warm water
2 tsp. salt	1/2 tsp. garlic powder
2 tbsp. butter	4 c. unsifted flour

Mix the milk, sugar, salt and butter in a bowl and cool to lukewarm. Dissolve the yeast in warm water, then stir into milk mixture. Add the garlic powder and flour and beat until blended. Cover and let rise in a warm place, free from draft, for about 40 minutes or until doubled in bulk. Stir down and beat for about 30 seconds. Turn into a greased 1 1/2-quart casserole. Bake in 375-degree oven for about 1 hour or until done.

Mrs. E. N. Harding, Jackson, Mississippi

CHEESE CASSEROLE BREAD

1 pkg. dry yeast	1/2 tsp. salt
1/4 c. warm water	1/3 c. butter or margarine
1/4 c. milk, scalded	1 egg, beaten
1 1/2 c. sifted flour	1/2 c. grated Parmesan cheese
1 tbsp. sugar	2 tbsp. chopped parsley

Dissolve the yeast in warm water. Cool the milk to lukewarm. Sift the flour, sugar and salt into a mixing bowl and cut in the butter until mixture resembles coarse meal. Add the egg, yeast and milk and beat well. Stir in the cheese and parsley and turn into a greased casserole. Cover with a damp cloth and let rise for about 40 minutes or until doubled in bulk. Dot with additional butter. Bake in 375-degree oven for 20 to 25 minutes or until done. Cut in pie-shaped wedges and serve hot. 8 servings.

Mrs. Jere Lyn Heitkamp, Normangee, Texas

VIRGINIA SALLY LUNN BREAD

4 eggs, well beaten	1/2 pkg. yeast
1/4 c. melted butter or	1 c. warm water
margarine	1/2 c. sugar
1 tsp. salt	5 c. sifted flour
1 c. lukewarm milk	

Mix the eggs, butter, salt, and milk in a bowl. Dissolve the yeast in warm water, then stir into egg mixture. Add the sugar and enough flour to make a stiff dough and beat well. Pour into a greased casserole and let rise for 6 to 7 hours. Bake at 350 degrees for 45 minutes. Serve hot with butter.

Mrs. Reginald L. Robinson, Fort Worth, Texas

CREOLE CASSEROLE BREAD

1 c. milk, scalded	2 pkg. dry yeast
3 tbsp. dark brown sugar	1 tsp. cinnamon
1 tbsp. salt	1/4 tsp. nutmeg
2 tbsp. margarine	4 c. unsifted flour
1 c. warm water	

Mix the milk, sugar, salt and margarine in a bowl and cool to lukewarm. Dissolve the yeast in warm water, then stir into milk mixture. Add the cinnamon, nutmeg and flour and stir until well blended. Cover and let rise in a warm place, free from draft, for about 1 hour or until doubled in bulk. Stir down and beat vigorously for 30 seconds. Turn into a greased 1 1/2-quart casserole. Bake in a 375-degree oven for about 1 hour or until done.

Mrs. Besse Miller, Perryton, Texas

MINUTE-SAVER CASSEROLE BREAD

2 c. warm water	2 tbsp. softened margarine
2 pkg. yeast	1/3 c. instant nonfat dry milk
3 tbsp. sugar	4 1/2 c. (about) unsifted flour
2 1/2 tsp. salt	

Pour the warm water into a large, warm bowl. Sprinkle with yeast and stir until dissolved. Stir in the sugar, salt, margarine, dry milk and half the flour and beat until smooth. Stir in enough remaining flour to make a stiff dough. Cover and let rise in a warm place, free from draft, for about 40 minutes or until more than doubled in bulk. Stir down and beat vigorously for about 30 seconds. Turn into a greased 1 1/2-quart casserole. Bake in 375-degree oven for about 45 minutes or until done. One teaspoon celery seed, 1/2 cup grated sharp Cheddar cheese, 2 teaspoons caraway seed or 3/4 cup seedless raisins may be added with second addition of flour, if desired.

PRIZE CASSEROLE BREAD

1 pkg. yeast	1 tbsp. soft butter
1/4 c. warm water	1 tbsp. dillseed
1 c. creamed cottage cheese	1 tsp. salt
1 egg, beaten	1 tsp. soda
1 tbsp. minced onion	2 to 2 1/2 c. flour

Dissolve the yeast in water in a bowl. Heat the cottage cheese to lukewarm, then stir into yeast. Add the egg, onion, butter, dillseed, salt and soda and mix. Stir in enough flour to form stiff dough. Cover and let rise in a warm place until doubled in bulk. Stir down and place in a well-greased 2-quart casserole. Let rise for 40 minutes. Bake at 350 degrees for 40 to 50 minutes. Slice thin and toast, if desired.

Mrs. James H. Davis, Houston, Texas

CASSEROLE PUMPERNICKEL BREAD

3 pkg. dry yeast	2 tbsp. soft shortening
1 1/2 c. warm water	2 3/4 c. rye flour
1/2 c. dark molasses	2 1/4 to 2 3/4 c. sifted flour
2 tbsp. caraway seed	Cornmeal
1 tbsp. salt	

Dissolve the yeast in warm water in a bowl. Add the molasses, caraway seed, salt, shortening, rye flour and 1 cup flour and beat until smooth. Add enough remaining flour to make a stiff dough. Turn out on a lightly floured surface and knead for 8 to 10 minutes or until smooth and elastic. Place in a greased bowl and turn to grease surface. Cover and let rise in a warm place for 1 hour and 30 minutes or until doubled in bulk. Stir down, then beat for about 30 seconds. Place in 2 greased casseroles sprinkled with cornmeal. Cover and let rise for about 30 minutes or until doubled in bulk. Bake at 375 degrees for 30 to 35 minutes or until well browned.

Natalie Preer, Wilmington, Delaware

PEASANT BREAD

2 pkg. dry yeast	2 tbsp. melted margarine
2 c. warm water	1 pkg. spaghetti sauce mix
2 tsp. salt	6 c. flour
2 tbsp. sugar	

Dissolve the yeast in warm water in a bowl. Blend the salt, sugar, margarine, sauce mix and half the flour. Add to the yeast and beat until smooth. Scrape down side of bowl, then beat in remaining flour until blended. Cover with a cloth and let rise in a warm place until doubled in bulk. Stir down and beat for 25 seconds. Turn into a greased 2-quart casserole. Bake in 375-degree oven for 1 hour. Remove to rack to cool.

Catherine Downs, Jackson, Tennessee

WHOLE WHEAT BATTER BREAD

1 c. milk, scalded	1 c. warm water
3 tbsp. sugar	2 1/4 c. unsifted whole wheat
1 tbsp. salt	flour
2 tbsp. margarine	2 c. unsifted flour
2 pkg. dry yeast	

Mix the milk, sugar, salt and margarine in a bowl and cool to lukewarm. Dissolve the yeast in warm water, then stir into milk mixture. Stir in the flours and beat until well blended. Cover and let rise for about 40 minutes or until doubled in bulk. Stir down and beat well. Turn into a greased casserole. Bake at 375 degrees for 50 minutes. Remove from casserole and brush with additional margarine.

Mrs. Allen Bryant, Frederick, Maryland

loaves & corn bread

QUICK BREADS

Time-conscious homemakers appreciate the fast and easy aspects of quick breads. You mix your dough or batter, pour it into prepared pans, and let it bake while you go about your other tasks. In less than an hour, a piping hot loaf of bread emerges from your oven — ready to elicit compliments from your impressed family!

Two all-time favorite southern quick breads are featured in this section: quick loaves and corn breads. Some of the recipes are almost as old as the South itself — Quick Sally Lunn ... Boston Brown Bread ... and Old Virginia Spoon Bread. Others contain a little bit of southern history — Crackling Bread, for instance, which was the imaginative creation of women who were confronted with few foodstuffs and many hungry people after the Civil War. Their thrifty blending of fat, cornmeal, and seasonings has grown into a regional favorite! There's even a recipe for Easy Mexican Corn Bread.

There are recipes for the traditional holiday and party breads, too, such as Banana Nut Bread, Date and Nut Loaf, and Cheddar Corn Bread. These are just a few of the flavorful, home-tested recipes you'll find in the pages of this section. They're favorites in homes throughout the Southland — and they're certain to become favorites in your home, too!

OLIVE BREAD

2 1/4 c. sifted flour	1/4 c. sugar
4 tsp. baking powder	1 egg, beaten
3/4 c. sliced pimento-stuffed	1 1/4 c. milk
olives	2 tbsp. melted butter

Preheat oven to 375 degrees. Sift the flour and baking powder together into a mixing bowl and add olives and sugar. Combine the egg, milk and butter. Add to dry ingredients and stir just enough to moisten flour. Place in a greased 5 x 9-inch loaf pan. Bake for about 1 hour or until bread tests done.

Mrs. Myrtle S. VonCannon, Greensboro, North Carolina

CHEESE-NUT BREAD

2 c. sifted flour	1/2 c. chopped pecans
1 tbsp. baking powder	1 egg, beaten
3/4 tsp. salt	3/4 c. milk
1/2 tsp. sugar	2 tbsp. melted butter
1 c. grated American cheese	

Sift the flour with baking powder, salt and sugar twice and place in a large bowl. Add the cheese and pecans and mix thoroughly. Mix the egg, milk and butter. Pour into dry ingredients and stir until dry ingredients are just dampened. Batter will be lumpy. Pour into a greased bread pan and let stand at room temperature for 15 minutes. Bake at 350 degrees for 1 hour or until toothpick inserted in center comes out clean. Cool before slicing.

Mrs. Henry J. H. Cooke, Norfolk, Virginia

QUICK SALLY LUNN BREAD

1/2 c. shortening	3 tsp. baking powder
1/2 c. sugar	3/4 tsp. salt
3 eggs	1 c. milk
2 c. sifted flour	

Cream the shortening and sugar in a bowl. Beat in the eggs, one at a time. Sift the flour with baking powder and salt and add to creamed mixture alternately with milk. Place in a greased 9 x 12-inch baking pan. Bake at 425 degrees for about 30 minutes. Cut into squares and serve hot. 6 servings.

Mrs. W. C. Lumpkin, Tuskegee, Alabama

AVOCADO-NUT BREAD

2 c. flour	1 egg, slightly beaten
1/2 tsp. soda	1/2 c. sour milk
3/4 c. sugar	1/2 c. mashed avocado
1/2 tsp. baking powder	1 c. chopped nuts
1/4 tsp. salt	

Sift the flour, soda, sugar, baking powder and salt together into a large bowl. Add the egg, milk, avocado and nuts and mix just enough to moisten dry ingredients. Pour into a greased 9 x 5 x 3-inch loaf pan. Bake at 350 degrees for 1 hour.

Mrs. F. T. Black, El Paso, Texas

SWEET ANISE BREAD

3 c. flour	2 eggs, beaten
4 1/2 tsp. baking powder	2 c. milk
1/2 tsp. salt	2 tbsp. melted butter
1/2 c. sugar	5 tsp. aniseed

Sift dry ingredients together into a bowl and stir in the eggs and milk. Add the butter and aniseed and beat well. Turn into 2 small well-greased loaf pans. Bake at 350 degrees for 30 minutes.

Rosemarie Preston, Enid, Oklahoma

BOSTON BROWN BREAD

4 c. sour milk	1 tsp. salt
3 tsp. soda	5 c. graham flour
3/4 c. sugar	1/2 c. flour
1 c. molasses	1 1/2 tsp. baking powder

Mix the milk, soda, sugar, molasses and salt in a large bowl. Add remaining ingredients and stir until well mixed. Pour into 3 greased loaf pans. Bake at 425 degrees for 10 minutes. Reduce temperature to 350 degrees and bake for 45 to 50 minutes longer.

Lynnie E. Oakes, Clermont, Florida

CHEDDAR BRAN LOAF

1 1/2 c. sifted flour	1/3 c. sugar
1 1/2 tsp. baking powder	1 egg, well beaten
1/4 tsp. soda	1 c. buttermilk
1/2 tsp. salt	1 c. shredded Cheddar cheese
3 tbsp. butter or margarine	1 c. crushed whole bran cereal

Sift the flour, baking powder, soda and salt together. Cream the butter and sugar in a bowl and blend in egg. Add the flour mixture alternately with buttermilk, beginning and ending with flour mixture. Fold in the cheese and cereal and spoon into well-greased 8 x 4-inch loaf pan. Bake in 350-degree oven for 1 hour. Remove from pan and cool.

Mrs. M. A. Berns, Norfolk, Virginia

APRICOT BREAD

2 c. sifted flour	3/4 c. crunchy nut-like cereal
1 c. sugar	nuggets
2 1/2 tsp. baking powder	1 1/4 c. milk
3/4 tsp. salt	1 egg, well beaten
1/2 c. chopped dried apricots	2 tbsp. melted shortening

Sift the flour with sugar, baking powder, and salt and stir in the apricots and cereal nuggets. Blend the milk with egg and shortening in a bowl. Add flour mixture and stir just until flour is moistened. Pour into a greased 9 x 5-inch loaf pan. Bake at 350 degrees for 1 hour and 15 minutes or until cake tester inserted into center comes out clean. Cool in the pan for 10 minutes. Remove from pan and finish cooling on rack. Wrap bread in waxed paper, plastic wrap or aluminum foil and store overnight for easier slicing.

Photograph for this recipe on page 5.

PINEAPPLE BREAD

1 3/4 c. unsifted flour	2 eggs, beaten
2 1/2 tsp. baking powder	1 8 1/2-oz. can crushed
1 tsp. salt	pineapple
3/4 tsp. cinnamon	1/3 c. milk
1/4 tsp. nutmeg	2 tbsp. molasses
1/8 tsp. allspice	1/4 c. melted shortening,
2/3 c. (firmly packed) light	cooled
brown sugar	1 1/2 c. crisp whole wheat
1/4 c. chopped nuts	flakes

Mix the flour, baking powder, salt and spices together in a bowl. Add the sugar and nuts and mix. Mix the eggs, undrained pineapple, milk, molasses and shortening. Add to flour mixture and mix just enough to moisten the flour. Stir in the cereal gently. Pour into a well-greased 5-cup ring mold. Bake at 350 degrees for 35 to 40 minutes or until cake tester inserted in center comes out clean. Cool for about 10 minutes, then turn out on a rack to finish cooling. Wrap in waxed paper or foil. Bread slices better the second day. Bread may be baked in an 8 x 4-inch loaf pan for 1 hour to 1 hour and 5 minutes.

Photograph for this recipe on page 5.

CRANBERRY-COCOA BREAD

1 1-lb. can whole cranberry sauce	2 tsp. soda
1 1/2 c. raisins	1 tsp. salt
Grated rind of 1 orange	1/4 c. cocoa
3 tbsp. butter or margarine	1 tsp. ground cinnamon
1 c. sugar	1/2 tsp. nutmeg
1 egg	1 c. chopped walnuts
1/3 c. milk	1 8-oz. package cream cheese
3 c. sifted all-purpose flour	1/4 c. cranberry juice

Combine the cranberry sauce, raisins and orange rind in a saucepan and cook over low heat, stirring constantly, for 5 minutes. Cool. Cream butter in a bowl until light and fluffy. Add the sugar gradually and cream well. Beat egg with milk and stir into butter mixture. Sift the flour with soda, salt, cocoa and spices and fold in walnuts. Add to creamed mixture alternately with cranberry mixture, blending well after each addition. Pour into well-greased 9 x 5 x 3-inch pan. Bake at 350 degrees for 45 minutes, then place tent of foil over top. Bake for 35 minutes longer or until bread tests done. Cool thoroughly. Mix the cream cheese with cranberry juice and spread on slices of bread.

Mrs. Nicole Riddle, Montgomery, Alabama

PEAR-NUT BREAD

1/2 c. salad oil	1 tsp. soda
1 c. sugar	1/4 tsp. ground cinnamon
2 eggs	1/4 tsp. ground nutmeg
1/4 c. sour cream	1/2 c. chopped walnuts
1 tsp. vanilla	1 c. chopped pared fresh
2 c. sifted all-purpose flour	California Bartlett pears
1/2 tsp. salt	

Beat the oil and sugar in a large bowl with electric mixer until well blended. Beat in the eggs, one at a time. Add sour cream and vanilla and beat well. Sift the flour, salt, soda, cinnamon and nutmeg together. Add to the sugar mixture and beat until well blended. Add walnuts and pears and stir well. Spoon into a well-greased 9 x 5-inch loaf pan. Bake at 350 degrees for 1 hour or until a toothpick inserted in center comes out clean. Cool in the pan for 10 to 15 minutes. Turn out on a rack and cool. Slice very thin and spread with softened butter or cream cheese, if desired.

CHEDDAR APPLE BREAD

1/2 c. shortening	1 tsp. soda
1/2 c. sugar	1 tsp. baking powder
1 egg	1 c. shredded Cheddar cheese
1 No. 2 can apple pie filling	1/2 c. chopped walnuts or
2 1/2 c. sifted flour	pecans
1 tsp. salt	

Cream the shortening and sugar in a bowl and add egg. Beat in apple pie filling. Sift the flour, salt, soda and baking powder together and add to creamed mixture. Add the cheese and walnuts and mix quickly. Pour into a well-greased 9 x 5-inch loaf pan. Bake at 350 degrees for 1 hour and 30 minutes.

APPLE-NUT BREAD

1/4 c. shortening	1/2 tsp. baking powder
1/2 c. sugar	1/2 tsp. soda
1 egg	1/4 tsp. salt
2/3 c. unsweetened applesauce	3 tbsp. sour milk
2 c. sifted flour	1/2 c. chopped nuts

Cream the shortening and sugar in a bowl, then stir in the egg. Stir in applesauce. Combine dry ingredients. Add to egg mixture and mix well. Stir in the sour milk and nuts and place in a greased loaf pan. Bake at 350 degrees for 45 minutes or until done.

Mrs. Elizabeth Fulghum, Sims, North Carolina

BANANA-NUT BREAD

1 1/2 c. sugar	1/2 tsp. soda
1/2 c. shortening	1/4 tsp. baking powder
2 lge. eggs	3 c. sifted flour
3 lge. bananas, mashed	1/2 c. finely chopped nuts
1/2 tsp. salt	

Cream the sugar and shortening in a bowl. Stir in the eggs and bananas. Add the salt, soda and baking powder to flour, then stir into the banana mixture. Fold in the nuts. Pour into 3 greased coffee cans. Bake at 325 degrees for about 1 hour.

Mrs. Ruby Eastham, Rush, Kentucky

CARROT BROWN BREAD

2 eggs	1 1/2 c. flour
1/2 c. molasses	2 1/2 tsp. soda
2 c. buttermilk	1 tsp. salt
2 c. graham flour	1 c. raisins or chopped dates
1/3 c. melted margarine	1 c. shredded carrots
1/2 c. sugar	

Beat the eggs well in a large bowl. Add molasses and buttermilk and stir well. Stir in 1 cup graham flour and margarine. Mix the sugar, flour, soda and salt and add to egg mixture, small amount at a time, stirring well after each addition. Mix in raisins and carrots and pour into 3 greased bread pans. Bake at 350 degrees for 40 to 45 minutes.

Mrs. Doris Miles, Ferguson, North Carolina

PEANUT-ORANGE BREAD

2 1/4 c. sifted all-purpose flour	1 egg, well beaten
3 tsp. baking powder	1 c. milk
1/2 tsp. salt	1 1/2 tsp. grated orange rind
1/3 c. sugar	1/4 c. chopped salted peanuts
1/2 c. peanut butter	

Sift the dry ingredients together into a bowl and cut in peanut butter. Mix the egg, milk and orange rind and stir into the flour mixture. Fold in the peanuts and pour into well-greased 9 x 5 x 3-inch loaf pan. Bake at 350 degrees for 35 to 40 minutes. Remove from pan and cool.

Mrs. LeRoy Butler, Atlanta, Georgia

CRANBERRY-BANANA-NUT BREAD

1/3 c. shortening	1/2 tsp. salt
2/3 c. sugar	1/2 c. coarsely chopped nuts
2 eggs	1 c. ripe mashed bananas
1 3/4 c. sifted flour	1 c. whole cranberry sauce,
2 tsp. baking powder	drained

Cream the shortening with sugar in a bowl and add eggs, one at a time, beating well after each addition. Sift dry ingredients together and add nuts. Add flour mixture to creamed mixture alternately with bananas, then fold in cranberry sauce. Pour into a greased loaf pan. Bake in 350-degree oven for about 1 hour or until done. Cool before slicing.

Mrs. Naomi Osborne, East Orange, Texas

CINNAMON CRUNCH WALNUT LOAF

1 1/2 c. coarsely chopped	4 1/2 tsp. baking powder
California walnuts	1 1/2 tsp. salt
1 tbsp. melted butter	1/4 c. shortening
1 c. sugar	1 egg
2 tsp. cinnamon	1 1/4 c. milk
3 c. sifted all-purpose flour	

Toss the walnuts with butter. Add 1/4 cup sugar and cinnamon and mix until walnuts are well coated. Set aside. Sift the flour with remaining sugar, baking powder and salt into a bowl and cut in shortening. Beat the egg lightly and combine with milk. Stir into flour mixture just until all the flour is moistened. Reserve 1/4 cup walnut mixture. Add remaining walnut mixture to batter and mix lightly. Spoon into a greased 9 1/4 x 5 1/4 x 2 3/4-inch loaf pan. Sprinkle with reserved walnut mixture and let stand for 15 minutes. Bake at 350 degrees for 1 hour and 5 minutes to 1 hour and 20 minutes or until loaf tests done. Let stand for 10 minutes. Turn out on a wire rack and cool.

Photograph for this recipe on page 58.

DATE AND NUT LOAF

1 pkg. pitted dates	3 c. flour
1 1/2 c. boiling water	1 tsp. soda
1/2 c. butter	1 tsp. cream of tartar
1 1/2 c. sugar	1 tsp. vanilla
1 tsp. salt	1 c. chopped nuts
2 eggs, beaten	

Chop the dates and place in a large bowl. Add the boiling water, butter, sugar and salt and set aside until cool. Add the eggs and mix. Sift the flour, soda and cream of tartar together. Add to the date mixture and mix well. Stir in the vanilla and nuts. Pour into a greased and floured loaf pan. Bake at 325 degrees for 1 hour.

Della Woeford, Irvine, Kentucky

LETTUCE LOAF

1 1/2 c. sifted flour	1 c. sugar
2 tsp. baking powder	1/2 c. cooking oil
1/2 tsp. soda	1 1/2 tsp. grated lemon rind
1/2 tsp. salt	1 c. finely chopped lettuce
1/8 tsp. ground mace	2 eggs
1/8 tsp. ground ginger	1/2 c. chopped nuts

Sift the flour, baking powder, soda, salt and spices together. Combine the sugar, oil and lemon rind in a bowl, then mix in flour mixture and lettuce. Add the eggs, one at a time, beating well after each addition. Stir in the nuts. Turn into a greased and floured 8 1/2 x 4 1/2 x 2 1/2-inch loaf pan. Bake at 350 degrees for 55 minutes. Cool in pan for 15 minutes. Remove from pan and cool on a wire rack.

Mrs. Montie Rae Carpenter, Brightwood, Virginia

ORANGE-DATE BREAD

1 stick margarine	1/2 c. orange juice
1/4 c. sugar	3 c. sifted flour
1/2 c. light brown sugar	2 tsp. baking powder
2 eggs, beaten	1/2 tsp. soda
1 tbsp. grated orange peel	1/2 tsp. salt
1/2 tsp. vanilla	1 c. chopped dates
1/2 c. sour milk	1 c. chopped nuts

Cream the margarine with sugars in a mixing bowl. Add the eggs, orange peel and vanilla and beat until light and fluffy. Add the sour milk and beat well. Add orange juice and beat thoroughly. Sift the flour, baking powder, soda and salt together. Add to creamed mixture and stir just until blended. Fold in dates and nuts and pour into a greased 9 x 5 x 3-inch loaf pan. Bake at 350 degrees for 1 hour to 1 hour and 10 minutes. Remove from pan and cool before slicing.

Mrs. Darrell E. Hager, Iron Station, North Carolina

PUMPKIN BREAD

3 c. sugar	1 tsp. nutmeg
4 eggs, beaten	2/3 c. water
1 c. salad oil	2 c. canned pumpkin
1 1/2 tsp. salt	3 1/2 c. flour
1 tsp. cinnamon	2 tsp. soda

Mix the sugar, eggs, oil, salt, cinnamon, nutmeg and water in a bowl. Add the pumpkin and mix well. Stir in the flour and soda. Place in 2 well-greased loaf pans. Bake at 350 degrees for 1 hour.

Mrs. Robert L. Fryer, Antioch, Tennessee

CURRIED CORNMEAL MUFFINS

1/4 c. chopped green onion	1 tbsp. baking powder
3 tbsp. vegetable oil	2 tbsp. sugar
1 1/4 c. cornmeal	1 tbsp. curry powder
3/4 c. sifted flour	1 egg, beaten
3/4 tsp. salt	1 c. milk

Preheat oven to 425 degrees. Cook the onion in oil until tender and set aside. Sift the cornmeal, flour, salt, baking powder, sugar and curry powder together into a bowl. Add the egg, milk and onion and stir until just mixed. Fill 12 greased medium muffin cups 2/3 full. Bake for 15 to 18 minutes. Serve hot.

CHEDDAR CORN BREAD

1 c. flour	2 eggs, beaten
1 c. yellow cornmeal	1 c. milk
1 tbsp. baking powder	2 c. shredded sharp
2 tbsp. salt	Cheddar cheese

Sift dry ingredients together into a bowl. Add the eggs, milk and cheese and stir just until blended. Pour into a hot, well-greased 1 1/2-quart ring mold. Bake at 425 degrees for 20 minutes. Center of corn bread may be filled with meat stew or creamed vegetable, if desired. 6 servings.

Mrs. A. Frank Arnold, Spruce Pine, North Carolina

CORN PONETTES

3/4 c. cornmeal	1 med. onion, grated
1/2 c. flour	1 egg, lightly beaten
2 tsp. baking powder	1 c. cream-style corn
1/4 tsp. salt	Dash of hot sauce

Sift the cornmeal, flour, baking powder and salt together into a mixing bowl. Mix the onion, egg, corn and hot sauce and stir into cornmeal mixture. Drop by rounded teaspoonfuls into small amount of hot fat in a skillet. Cook until golden brown on both sides and drain on absorbent paper. 6-8 servings.

Mrs. B. R. Coley, Lithonia, Georgia

CRACKLING BREAD

2 c. cornmeal	2 c. sour milk
1/2 tsp. soda	2 eggs, well beaten
2 tsp. baking powder	1 c. chopped cracklings
2 tsp. salt	

Sift the dry ingredients together into a bowl. Add the milk, eggs and cracklings and mix well. Pour into a hot, greased skillet. Bake at 400 degrees for about 30 minutes or until done.

Mrs. Roy McMurry, Sandy Hook, Mississippi

EASY MEXICAN CORN BREAD

1 c. white cornmeal	1 c. sour milk
1/2 tsp. salt	2 eggs, beaten
1/2 tsp. soda	1/3 c. minced jalapeno pepper
1 c. yellow cream-style corn	1 c. grated Cheddar cheese
1/2 c. vegetable oil	2 tbsp. shortening

Mix the cornmeal, salt and soda in a bowl. Add the corn, oil, milk and eggs and mix well. Stir in the jalapeno pepper and cheese and mix. Melt the shortening in a large iron skillet and pour the cornmeal mixture into the skillet. Bake at 350 degrees for about 35 minutes or until done.

Mrs. Ray Kimbrell, Warren, Arkansas

PUMPKIN GRIDDLE BREAD

2 c. cooked pumpkin	1 tbsp. sugar
1/2 c. (about) cornmeal	1/8 lb. melted butter
1/2 tsp. salt	

Mix the pumpkin, cornmeal, salt, sugar and butter in a bowl. Batter should be medium-stiff. Drop by spoonfuls on a greased, hot griddle and cook until brown. Turn and brown on other side.

Lola A. Harris, Shelbyville, Kentucky

HUSH PUPPIES

1 3/4 c. cornmeal	1 tsp. salt
1/4 c. flour	3 tbsp. finely chopped onion
1/2 tsp. soda	1 c. buttermilk
1 tsp. baking powder	1 egg, beaten

Mix the dry ingredients in a bowl and stir in the onion, then buttermilk. Add the egg and mix well. Drop by spoonfuls into deep, hot fat and fry until golden brown. Drain on absorbent paper.

Mrs. John White, Dalton, Georgia

JOHNNYCAKES

1 c. cornmeal	1 1/2 tbsp. melted shortening
2 tbsp. flour	1 c. boiling milk
1/2 tsp. salt	1 egg, separated
1 tbsp. sugar	

Sift the cornmeal and flour together and spread on a baking sheet. Bake at 275 degrees until lightly browned. Mix the cornmeal mixture, salt and sugar in a bowl. Add the shortening, milk and egg yolk and mix well. Beat the egg white until stiff and fold into cornmeal mixture. Drop from a spoon into greased baking pan, leaving 1/2 inch between each cake. Bake at 400 degrees for 30 minutes. 12 cakes.

Mrs. Ellie Hayes, Benson, North Carolina

OLD VIRGINIA SPOON BREAD

1 1/2 c. boiling water	1 c. buttermilk
1 c. self-rising cornmeal	1 tsp. sugar
1 tbsp. butter	1/4 tsp. soda
3 eggs, separated	

Stir the boiling water into cornmeal in a bowl, then cool slightly. Add the butter and egg yolks and stir until thoroughly blended. Stir in the buttermilk, sugar and soda. Beat the egg whites until soft peaks form, then fold into cornmeal mixture. Pour into a greased 2-quart casserole. Bake in 375-degree oven for 45 to 50 minutes. Serve hot with butter. 4-6 servings.

Mrs. Emmett Crockett, Murfreesboro, Tennessee

SOUTHERN TOMATO SPOON BREAD

1 c. cornmeal	2 c. milk, scalded
1 c. tomato juice	1/4 c. butter or margarine

1 sm. onion, grated
1 tsp. baking powder

3/4 tsp. salt
3 eggs, separated

Mix the cornmeal with tomato juice. Stir into the milk in a saucepan slowly and cook until thick, stirring frequently. Remove from heat and stir in the butter, onion, baking powder and salt. Add to the beaten egg yolks gradually, stirring vigorously to blend. Beat the egg whites until stiff but not dry and fold into cornmeal mixture. Turn into a greased 1 1/2-quart baking dish. Bake in 375-degree oven for 40 to 50 minutes or until a knife inserted in center comes out clean.

Mrs. G. B. Powell, Birmingham, Alabama

VEGETABLE SPOON BREAD

1 c. cornmeal
1 1/2 tsp. salt
1 c. cold milk
1 1/2 c. scalded milk
1 tbsp. butter or margarine

1 1-lb. can mixed vegetables, drained
5 slices cooked bacon, crumbled
4 eggs, separated

Preheat oven to 350 degrees. Combine the cornmeal, salt and cold milk. Add to scalded milk and cook for about 5 minutes or until thickened, stirring constantly. Remove from heat. Add the butter, vegetables and bacon and mix well. Beat the egg yolks until thick and lemon-colored. Stir a small amount of cornmeal mixture into egg yolks, then stir back into cornmeal mixture. Fold in stiffly beaten egg whites. Pour into a greased 2-quart casserole. Bake for 50 to 60 minutes. Serve immediately.

biscuits
& muffins

QUICK BREADS

No meal in a southern home would be complete without a basket full of finger-burning hot biscuits or muffins. These delightful morsels are used to absorb gravy or meat drippings, to accent the flavor of a certain dish, or are enjoyed for their own delicious taste. Preparing a pan of biscuits or muffins is often one of the first things a southern homemaker does in the morning — and her happy family then enjoys biscuits or muffins with their breakfast. What a great way to start the day!

Every homemaker has her own favorite recipe for these treats — and the very best of these family-tested recipes are shared with you in the pages that follow. Serve your family biscuits with supper tonight — take your pick from Brown Honey Biscuits . . . Cornmeal Biscuits . . . Old-Fashioned Vinegar Rolls . . . or one of the oldest and most-loved biscuit recipes, Southern Drop Biscuits.

And why not give your family a special lift in the morning by serving warm muffins. Choose your favorite from Bacon Corn Bread Muffins . . . Blueberry Muffins . . . Country Breakfast Muffins . . . or any of the many recipes you'll find as you browse through the pages that follow. Start a new tradition in your home by serving biscuits or muffins. You'll be glad you did!

73

BISCUITS

3 c. flour	3/4 tsp. cream of tartar
4 1/2 tsp. baking powder	3/4 c. shortening
2 1/2 tbsp. sugar	1 c. milk
3/4 tsp. salt	1 egg (opt.)

Place the flour in a 2-quart bowl. Add the baking powder, sugar, salt and cream of tartar and toss lightly. Cut in the shortening with pastry blender until mixture is consistency of peas. Make a well in center and pour in half the milk. Mix well. Add the egg and remaining milk and mix lightly. Turn out on a lightly floured surface and roll to 1/2 to 3/4-inch thickness. Cut with lightly floured 2-inch biscuit cutter and place on a cookie sheet. Bake at 400 degrees for 12 to 15 minutes or until lightly browned.

Mrs. Alan Walter, Beaufort, South Carolina

BROWN HONEY BISCUITS

1 c. whole wheat flour	1/4 c. shortening
1 c. flour	1 tbsp. honey
4 tsp. baking powder	1/2 to 2/3 c. water
1/2 tsp. salt	

Mix the whole wheat flour, flour, baking powder and salt in a bowl. Cut in the shortening until mixture is consistency of cornmeal. Add the honey and enough water to make a soft dough and mix well. Roll out on a floured board to 1/2 to 3/8-inch thickness. Cut with a biscuit cutter and place on a cookie sheet. Bake at 400 degrees for about 15 minutes or until brown.

Mrs. Blaine B. Campbell, Laredo, Texas

BUTTERMILK BISCUITS

2 c. flour	1/2 tsp. cream of tartar
1 tbsp. baking powder	1/4 c. shortening
3/4 tsp. salt	1 c. buttermilk
1/2 tsp. soda	1 stick butter or margarine

Sift dry ingredients together twice and place in a mixing bowl. Cut in the shortening until well mixed. Add the buttermilk and stir well. Drop by tablespoons onto greased cookie sheet and place a pat of butter on each biscuit. Bake at 450 degrees for 10 minutes. 26 biscuits.

Mrs. James E. Shotts, Jasper, Alabama

EASY BISCUITS

2 c. sifted self-rising flour	2/3 c. (about) milk
3 tbsp. shortening	

Place the flour in a bowl and cut in shortening until mixture is consistency of cornmeal. Add enough milk to make a soft dough and mix well. Turn out on a lightly floured board and knead lightly for 30 seconds. Roll out 1/2 inch thick. Cut with a 2-inch biscuit cutter and place on a baking sheet. Bake in 450-degree oven for 10 to 12 minutes.

Mrs. Jim Whitledge, Clay, Kentucky

CHEESE BISCUITS

1 1/4 c. sifted flour	1/3 c. grated sharp cheese
1/2 c. yellow cornmeal	1/4 c. shortening
3 tsp. baking powder	1/2 to 3/4 c. milk
1/2 tsp. salt	

Combine the flour, cornmeal, baking powder and salt in a bowl and cut in the cheese and shortening until mixture resembles coarse crumbs. Add the milk and stir until mixed. Knead on a floured board and roll out 1/2 inch thick. Cut with a biscuit cutter and place on an ungreased cookie sheet. Bake in 450-degree oven for 10 to 12 minutes.

K. B. McElroy, Hugo, Oklahoma

CORNMEAL BISCUITS

3/4 c. milk, scalded	1 tsp. salt
1/2 c. cornmeal	1/4 c. shortening
1 1/2 c. flour	Melted butter
4 tsp. baking powder	

Mix the milk and cornmeal well. Sift the flour, baking powder and salt together into a bowl. Add the shortening and mix thoroughly. Add the cornmeal mixture and mix well. Knead on a floured board until smooth. Roll out thin and cut with a floured biscuit cutter. Brush tops with melted butter and stack 2 biscuits together. Place on a greased baking sheet. Bake at 425 degrees for about 15 minutes. 24 biscuits.

Mrs. Leon Dixon, Waynesboro, Tennessee

CREAM CRACKERS

1 1/2 c. flour	3 tbsp. butter
1/2 tsp. salt	

Preheat oven to 475 degrees. Sift the flour and salt together into a bowl and cut in the butter. Stir in just enough water to moisten flour. Roll out very thin on a floured surface. Fold into thirds, then roll out very thin again. Cut into squares and place on a baking sheet. Place on top rack of oven. Bake for about 7 minutes.

Judith Bowen, Cumberland, Maryland

COTTAGE CHEESE BISCUITS

3 c. flour
3 tsp. baking powder
1/4 tsp. salt
1 tbsp. sugar
1/4 c. shortening

1/2 c. milk
2 eggs, beaten
1 c. cottage cheese
1 egg yolk, beaten

Sift the flour, baking powder, salt and sugar together into a bowl. Cut in the shortening until consistency of meal. Stir in the milk, eggs and cottage cheese. Turn out on a floured board and knead lightly. Roll to desired thickness and cut with a biscuit cutter. Brush with egg yolk and place on a cookie sheet. Bake in 425-degree oven for 20 to 25 minutes. 16 biscuits.

Mrs. Don Jackson, Chesapeake, Virginia

CRANBERRY TEA BISCUITS

2 c. sifted all-purpose flour
3 tsp. baking powder
1/4 tsp. soda
1 tsp. salt
3 tbsp. shortening

1 c. jellied cranberry sauce
1 egg, beaten
1/4 c. sour cream
1/2 c. grated cheese

Sift the dry ingredients together into a bowl and cut in shortening. Mash the cranberry sauce in a bowl. Add the egg and sour cream and mix well. Add to flour mixture and mix well. Roll out on floured board to a rectangle and cut in small squares. Sprinkle with cheese. Place on a baking sheet. Bake at 400 degrees for 15 to 20 minutes.

Mrs. Earl L. Faulkenberry, Lancaster, South Carolina

FRIED EGG BISCUITS

8 to 10 cold biscuits
2 eggs, beaten

2 tbsp. milk
Salt and pepper to taste

Cut the biscuits into halves. Mix the eggs, milk, salt and pepper in a bowl. Dip biscuit halves in egg mixture and drain lightly. Fry in a small amount of hot fat in a skillet until brown on both sides.

Mrs. Augustus Collins, Mullins, South Carolina

EDNA'S BISCUITS

2 c. flour
1/2 tsp. salt
1 tsp. baking powder

1/2 tsp. soda
3 tbsp. shortening
3/4 to 1 c. buttermilk

Sift the flour, salt, baking powder and soda together into a bowl and cut in shortening. Add enough buttermilk for a soft dough and mix until blended. Roll out 3/8 inch thick on a floured surface and cut with a biscuit cutter. Place on a cookie sheet. Bake in 475-degree oven for 12 to 15 minutes. 10 biscuits.

Mrs. Edna Clore, Brightwood, Virginia

BLUEBERRY BISCUITS

2 c. sifted flour	1/3 c. butter
3 tsp. baking powder	1 egg
1 tsp. salt	1/3 c. buttermilk
2 tbsp. sugar	1 c. fresh blueberries

Sift the flour, baking powder, salt and sugar together into a bowl. Cut in the butter with 2 knives or a pastry blender. Reserve 1 tablespoon unbeaten egg white. Mix remaining egg and buttermilk. Add to flour mixture and mix just enough to moisten dry ingredients. Fold in the blueberries. Turn out on a lightly floured board and pat to 1/4 to 1/2 inch thickness. Cut into squares, triangles or diamonds with a floured knife. Mix the reserved egg white with 1 teaspoon water and brush on biscuits. Sprinkle with additional sugar. Place on a cookie sheet. Bake at 425 degrees for 10 to 15 minutes. Serve with additional butter and blueberry jelly, if desired. 15-20 biscuits.

RAISIN-PEANUT COFFEE MUFFINS

2 c. sifted flour
3 tsp. baking powder
1 tsp. salt
2/3 c. sugar
1/2 c. mixed shortening and
  margarine
1 tsp. grated lemon peel
2 eggs, beaten

2/3 c. milk
1/2 c. chopped dark seedless
  raisins
1/2 c. peanut butter
2 tbsp. brown sugar
1/4 c. whole raisins
1 tbsp. melted butter

Sift the flour, baking powder, salt and sugar together into a bowl. Cut in the shortening mixture and lemon peel until mixture is consistency of cornmeal. Add the eggs, milk and chopped raisins and stir just until blended. Fill well-greased large muffin cups 2/3 full. Blend remaining ingredients in a saucepan and heat through. Drop by spoonfuls into muffin cups and swirl with a knife. Bake at 425 degrees for 20 to 25 minutes. Serve hot. 12 muffins.

Photograph for this recipe on page 72.

EVER-READY BISCUIT MIX

12 c. sifted flour
4 tbsp. baking powder

2 tbsp. salt
2 c. shortening

Sift flour, 3 cups at a time, adding 1 tablespoon baking powder and 1 1/2 teaspoons salt for each 3-cup amount, into a large bowl. Cut in the shortening with a pastry blender or 2 knives until mixture resembles coarse meal. Place in a glass jar and cover lightly with a cloth or plate. Store in refrigerator or cool, dry place. Keeps well for 3 to 4 weeks. Two cups biscuit mix and about 1/2 cup milk may be mixed to make 10 to 12 biscuits.

Mrs. Opal Storey, Newark, Delaware

SWEET POTATO BISCUITS

2 c. sifted flour
4 tsp. baking powder
1 tsp. salt
2/3 c. sugar

1/2 c. shortening
2 c. mashed sweet potatoes
1/4 c. milk

Sift the flour, baking powder, salt and sugar together into a bowl and cut in shortening until mixture is consistency of cornmeal. Mix in the sweet potatoes. Add the milk and mix well. Turn out on a floured board and knead lightly. Roll out to 1/2-inch thickness and cut with a 2-inch biscuit cutter. Place on a greased cookie sheet. Bake in 475-degree oven for 12 to 15 minutes. Serve hot with butter.

Mrs. Sam Hill, Morrilton, Arkansas

OLD-FASHIONED VINEGAR ROLLS

3/4 c. cider vinegar	1 tsp. salt
1 1/2 c. water	1/3 c. shortening
1 1/4 c. sugar	3/4 c. milk
4 tsp. cinnamon	4 tbsp. butter or margarine
2 c. sifted flour	Coffee cream
1 tbsp. baking powder	

Combine the vinegar, water, 1 cup sugar and 2 teaspoons cinnamon in a sauce-pan and stir over low heat until sugar is dissolved. Cook over medium heat for 20 minutes. Sift the flour, baking powder and salt together into a bowl and cut in shortening. Stir in milk and mix well. Roll out on floured surface into rectangle about 1/4 inch thick. Combine remaining sugar and cinnamon and sprinkle over rectangle. Dot with 2 tablespoons butter. Roll as for jelly roll, starting at long side. Cut crosswise into 1 1/4-inch slices and place, cut side up, close together in deep baking dish. Dot with remaining butter. Pour hot vinegar mixture over all. Bake at 375 degrees for 30 to 40 minutes and serve hot with cream. 8 servings.

Mrs. A. C. Ross, Flomaton, Alabama

SOUTHERN DROP BISCUITS

2 c. flour	1/2 tsp. cream of tartar
1 tbsp. baking powder	4 tbsp. shortening
3/4 tsp. salt	1 c. buttermilk
1/2 tsp. soda	1 stick butter or margarine

Sift dry ingredients together twice and place in a bowl. Cut in the shortening until well mixed. Add the buttermilk and stir well. Drop by tablespoonfuls onto greased cookie sheet. Place a pat of butter on each biscuit. Bake at 450 degrees for 10 minutes.

Mrs. James E. Shotts, Jasper, Alabama

NEW-FASHIONED BISCUITS

2 c. flour	3/4 c. milk
4 tsp. baking powder	1/2 c. mayonnaise
1 tsp. salt	1 tsp. grated lemon rind (opt.)
1 tbsp. sugar	

Sift dry ingredients together into a bowl and stir in milk, mayonnaise and lemon rind. Knead on a floured surface for 1 minute. Roll out and cut with a biscuit cutter. Place on a cookie sheet. Bake at 450 degrees for 12 minutes or until done. Serve hot.

Mrs. Flo Ponder, Ruston, Louisiana

WALNUT-LEMON MUFFINS

1 3/4 c. sifted all-purpose flour	1 egg
Sugar	2/3 c. milk
3 tsp. baking powder	1 tsp. grated lemon peel
1 tsp. salt	1 tbsp. lemon juice
2/3 c. chopped California walnuts	1/3 c. melted shortening
	California walnut halves

Sift the flour with 1/2 cup sugar, baking powder and salt into a bowl and add the chopped walnuts. Beat the egg lightly and add the milk, 1/2 teaspoon lemon peel, lemon juice and shortening. Add to the flour mixture and stir just until dry ingredients are moistened. Spoon into greased 2 1/2-inch muffin cups. Mix 3 tablespoons sugar with remaining lemon peel and sprinkle on muffins. Top each muffin with a walnut half. Bake at 400 degrees for about 20 minutes or until brown. Let stand for 2 minutes, then remove from pan carefully. Serve warm. 1 dozen.

BANANA MUFFINS

1/2 c. shortening	2 1/2 c. flour
1 c. sugar	2 1/2 tsp. soda
1 c. mashed bananas	1/2 tsp. salt
2 eggs, lightly beaten	

Cream the shortening with sugar in a bowl and add bananas. Add the eggs and mix well. Sift dry ingredients together and stir into batter. Pour into greased muffin pans. Bake at 350 degrees for 20 to 25 minutes.

Mrs. Eric Brown, Tullos, Louisiana

APPLE-CORNMEAL MUFFINS

1/2 c. flour	1 egg, well beaten
1 c. cornmeal	1/2 to 2/3 c. milk
1/2 tsp. salt	2 tbsp. melted butter
1 tbsp. sugar	1/2 c. finely chopped apples
2 1/2 tsp. baking powder	

Sift the flour, cornmeal, salt, sugar and baking powder together into a bowl. Add the egg and enough milk to make a medium batter and mix well. Add the butter and apples and mix thoroughly. Place in well-greased muffin tins. Bake in 400-degree oven for 20 to 25 minutes.

Ruby Faye Taylor, Pleasant Plains, Arkansas

BLUEBERRY MUFFINS

2 c. sifted all-purpose flour	2 eggs
1 1/2 tsp. baking powder	1 tsp. vanilla
1/2 tsp. salt	1/2 c. milk
1/2 c. soft butter or shortening	1 c. blueberries, floured
1 c. sugar	

Preheat oven to 375 degrees. Sift the flour, baking powder and salt together. Place the butter, sugar, eggs and vanilla in a bowl and beat with mixer at high speed until light and fluffy. Beat in flour mixture alternately with milk with mixer at low speed, beginning and ending with flour mixture. Beat until smooth. Fold in blueberries and fill muffin cups about 2/3 full. Bake for 20 to 25 minutes and serve warm.

Pearle Webb, Pineola, North Carolina

CHEESE MUFFINS

1 c. sifted self-rising flour	1 c. milk
1 c. self-rising cornmeal	1 egg
1/4 c. sugar	2 tbsp. melted shortening
2/3 c. grated cheese	

Combine the dry ingredients in a bowl and add cheese. Combine the milk, egg and shortening. Add to cheese mixture and stir to blend thoroughly. Spoon into hot, greased muffin cups. Bake at 400 degrees for about 20 minutes.

Mrs. R. L. Fleming, Austell, Georgia

BACON CORN BREAD MUFFINS

1 3/4 c. cornmeal	1 egg, beaten
1 tsp. salt	1 1/2 c. buttermilk
1 tsp. sugar	4 strips crisply cooked bacon,
1 tsp. baking powder	crumbled
1/2 tsp. soda	

Preheat oven to 450 degrees. Mix the dry ingredients in a bowl. Add egg and buttermilk and mix. Add the bacon and mix. Fill greased muffin cups 2/3 full. Bake for 15 minutes or until golden brown.

Jane Hunt Clark, Lexington, Kentucky

BRAN REFRIGERATOR MUFFINS

2 c. whole bran cereal with	1 qt. buttermilk
wheat germ	5 c. flour
2 c. boiling water	5 tsp. soda
1 c. butter or shortening	1 tbsp. salt
3 c. sugar	2 c. raisins (opt.)
4 eggs, well beaten	4 c. whole bran cereal

Mix the cereal with wheat germ and boiling water and let stand for 1 minute. Cream the butter and sugar in a bowl. Add eggs and buttermilk and mix well. Mix in the bran cereal mixture. Mix the flour, soda and salt and stir into the butter mixture. Add the raisins and bran cereal and stir until just mixed. Place in greased muffin tins. Bake at 400 degrees for 20 minutes. Place any remaining batter in refrigerator. May be stored up to 1 month. 4 quarts.

Mrs. Walter K. Wojcik, Yuma, Arizona

BASIC CORNMEAL MUFFINS

1 c. cornmeal	1/2 tsp. soda
1/2 c. flour	1 c. buttermilk
1 tsp. baking powder	1 egg
1/2 tsp. salt	Liquid vegetable shortening

Preheat oven to 450 degrees. Place the cornmeal in a mixing bowl. Sift the flour, baking powder, salt and soda together and add to cornmeal. Add the buttermilk and beat well. Add the egg and mix well. Place 1 teaspoon vegetable shortening in each cup of a muffin pan. Place the muffin pan in oven until smoking hot. Fill muffin cups 2/3 full with cornmeal mixture. Bake for 15 to 20 minutes.

Mrs. S. A. Wall, Fort Worth, Texas

BREAKFAST OAT MUFFINS

1 c. buttermilk	1 c. flour
1 c. quick-cooking oats	1 tsp. salt
1 egg, well beaten	1 tsp. baking powder
1/2 c. brown sugar	1/2 tsp. soda
1/3 c. (packed) salad oil	

Mix the buttermilk and oats in a bowl and refrigerate overnight. Add the egg, brown sugar and oil and mix well. Sift the flour, salt, baking powder and soda together and stir into oats mixture. Place in greased muffin tins. Bake at 400 degrees for 15 to 20 minutes. 12 muffins.

Mrs. Frances Rampey, Mount Pleasant, South Carolina

HONEY-PECAN BUNS

3 c. sifted flour	1/3 c. (firmly packed) light
3 tsp. baking powder	brown sugar
1 tsp. salt	1 1/2 tsp. cinnamon
1/3 c. sugar	1/2 tsp. grated orange rind
1/2 c. butter	3 tbsp. melted butter
1 c. evaporated milk	1/3 c. honey
1 egg, beaten	2/3 c. chopped pecans

Preheat oven to 425 degrees. Sift the flour, baking powder, salt and sugar together into a large mixing bowl. Cut in the butter until mixture resembles cornmeal. Add the milk and egg and stir until mixed. Turn out onto a well-floured surface and knead for 1 minute. Roll into a 10 x 15-inch rectangle. Mix the brown sugar, cinnamon, orange rind, melted butter and honey in a small bowl and spread half the mixture over dough. Sprinkle with 1/3 cup pecans. Roll as for jelly roll. Cut in 1-inch slices and place, cut side down, in lightly greased muffin cups. Top with remaining honey mixture and sprinkle with remaining pecans. Bake for 20 minutes. 20 buns.

COUNTRY BREAKFAST MUFFINS

1 egg	1 1/3 c. sifted flour
2 tbsp. sugar	1 tsp. baking powder
1 c. sour cream	1/2 tsp. soda
1 tbsp. soft shortening	1/2 tsp. salt

Beat the egg in a bowl until light. Add the sugar, sour cream and shortening and stir well. Stir in the flour, baking powder, soda and salt. Fill greased muffin cups 2/3 full. Bake at 400 degrees for 20 to 25 minutes or until golden brown. Serve hot. 12 medium muffins.

Shannon McCraw, Mize, Mississippi

DOUBLE CORN MUFFINS

1 c. sifted flour	1 egg, beaten
2 tbsp. sugar	1 8 3/4-oz. can cream-style
2 tsp. baking powder	corn
3/4 tsp. salt	3/4 c. milk
1 c. yellow cornmeal	2 tbsp. salad oil

Sift the flour, sugar, baking powder and salt together into a bowl and stir in cornmeal. Combine the egg, corn, milk and oil. Add to dry ingredients and stir just until moistened. Fill greased 2-inch muffin cups 2/3 full. Bake at 425 degrees for 30 minutes until golden brown. 20 muffins.

Mrs. Hugh E. Miller, Bristol, Tennessee

EASY CHEESY MUFFINS

1 c. sifted self-rising flour	1 c. milk
1 c. self-rising cornmeal	1 egg, beaten
1/4 c. sugar	2 tbsp. melted shortening
2/3 c. grated cheese	

Combine the dry ingredients in a bowl and add cheese. Combine the milk, egg and shortening. Add to cheese mixture and blend thoroughly. Place in hot, greased muffin cups. Bake at 425 degrees for about 20 minutes.

Mrs. R. L. Fleming, Austell, Georgia

EGGLESS CORN MUFFINS

1 1/8 c. flour	2 tbsp. sugar
1 1/8 c. cornmeal	1 tsp. baking powder
1/2 tsp. soda	1 1/2 c. sour milk
1/2 tsp. salt	1 tbsp. melted shortening

Sift dry ingredients together into a bowl. Add the sour milk and shortening and beat thoroughly. Fill greased muffin cups 1/2 full. Bake at 400 degrees for 25 minutes.

Mrs. Homer D. Baxter, Charleston, West Virginia

GRITS-CORNMEAL MUFFINS

1 c. milk	1/2 tsp. salt
1 egg	2 tsp. baking powder
1 c. cold cooked grits	1 1/4 c. cornmeal
1 tbsp. melted shortening	

Mix the milk, egg and grits in a bowl until blended. Add the shortening and remaining ingredients and mix well. Place in well-greased muffin cups. Bake at 425 degrees for about 25 minutes. 12 muffins.

Mrs. Bill Jones, Americus, Georgia

HERBED CORN GEMS

2 c. self-rising cornmeal	1 egg, lightly beaten
1/2 tsp. salt	2 tsp. grated onion
1/4 tsp. thyme	1/2 c. sour cream
1/2 tsp. celery seed	2 tbsp. melted shortening

Sift first 3 ingredients together into a bowl. Add the celery seed, egg, onion and sour cream and mix well. Stir in the shortening. Place in lightly greased muffin cups. Bake at 450 degrees for 20 minutes. Serve hot. Undiluted evaporated milk may be substituted for sour cream.

Mrs. J. O. Honeycutt, Gardendale, Alabama

MUSHROOM MUFFINS

1 4-oz. can mushroom stems and pieces	3 tsp. baking powder
1 tsp. butter	1 egg, beaten
2 c. flour	3/4 c. milk
1/4 c. sugar	1/2 c. grated American cheese
1 tsp. salt	1/4 c. melted shortening

Drain the mushrooms and reserve 1/4 cup liquid. Saute the mushrooms in butter in a saucepan for about 3 minutes. Sift dry ingredients together into a large bowl. Mix the egg, mushrooms, reserved mushroom liquid, milk, cheese and shortening and stir into flour mixture. Fill greased muffin cups 2/3 full. Bake at 400 degrees for 20 to 25 minutes.

Mrs. Victor Kruppenbacher, Orlando, Florida

PEANUT-ORANGE BREAKFAST PUFFS

2 c. sifted flour
1 tbsp. baking powder
1 tsp. salt
1/2 c. sugar
1 egg, beaten
1 c. milk

1/4 c. peanut oil
1/2 c. chopped salted peanuts
1 tsp. grated orange rind
1/4 c. melted butter or
    margarine

Sift the flour, baking powder, salt and 1/4 cup sugar together into a bowl. Combine the egg, milk and peanut oil. Add to flour mixture all at once and stir just until flour is moistened. Stir in the peanuts. Fill greased muffin cups 2/3 full. Bake in 425-degree oven for 15 to 20 minutes or until lightly browned. Blend remaining sugar and orange rind in a bowl. Dip hot muffin tops in melted butter, then in sugar mixture. Serve warm. 12 medium muffins.

PEANUT CANDY BUNS

2 tbsp. butter or margarine
1/4 c. flaked coconut
1/2 c. crushed peanut brittle

1 12-count pkg. refrigerator
biscuits

Preheat oven to 450 degrees. Measure 1/2 teaspoon butter into each of 12 medium muffin cups. Place the muffin pan in oven until butter is melted. Remove from oven and spoon 1 teaspoon coconut, then 2 teaspoons peanut brittle into each cup. Top with biscuits. Bake for 10 to 12 minutes or until biscuits are brown. Turn out immediately onto wire rack or bread board. Serve hot.

HOMINY GRITS MUFFINS

1 c. cold cooked hominy grits	4 tsp. baking powder
1 c. milk	1/2 tsp. salt
1 c. flour	2 eggs, well beaten

Mix the grits and milk in a bowl. Sift flour, baking powder and salt together and stir into grits mixture. Stir in the eggs and place in well-greased muffin tins. Bake at 400 degrees for 30 minutes.

Mrs. George S. Quillin, Fayetteville, North Carolina

MAPLE-CORN MUFFINS

1 egg, beaten	3/4 c. all-purpose flour
1/3 c. milk	1 1/2 tsp. baking powder
2 tbsp. maple syrup	1/4 tsp. salt
1/2 c. yellow cornmeal	3 tbsp. melted butter

Mix the egg, milk and syrup. Mix the cornmeal, flour, baking powder and salt in a bowl and stir in syrup mixture gradually. Add the butter and mix. Fill well-greased hot muffin cups 3/4 full. Bake at 425 degrees for 15 minutes or until brown. Serve hot with butter and maple syrup, if desired. 1 dozen.

Hedy Laniar, San Antonio, Texas

MAYONNAISE-CORNMEAL MUFFINS

2 c. cornmeal	1 egg
1 tsp. baking powder	1 tbsp. mayonnaise
1 tsp. salt	1 1/2 c. milk

Sift the cornmeal, baking powder and salt together into a bowl. Add the egg, mayonnaise and milk and beat well. Fill greased muffin cups 2/3 full. Bake in 400-degree oven for 25 minutes.

Mrs. Carl Kidd, Maryville, Tennessee

MAYONNAISE-SESAME MUFFINS

2 tsp. mayonnaise	1 c. milk
2 c. self-rising flour	2 tbsp. toasted sesame seed
2 tsp. sugar	

Mix the mayonnaise and flour in a bowl. Add the sugar and milk and mix well. Place in 12 greased muffin cups and sprinkle with sesame seed. Bake at 400 degrees for 20 minutes.

Mildred Fowler, Woodruff, South Carolina

doughnuts & coffee cakes

QUICK BREADS

When you want to mark a brunch as special or to serve a particularly festive bread for snacks, your thoughts almost always turn to doughnuts and coffee cakes. These flavor-packed breads are nearly as much fun to prepare as they are to eat! Using the quick bread recipes you'll find in this section, you can serve doughnuts and coffee cakes whenever you want to — with a minimum of effort.

Doughnuts are everyone's favorites — and this section contains the most popular family-acclaimed recipes from *Southern Living* homemakers. Bring warm, praises your way when you carry a platter heaped with doughnuts to your table. It's easy with these recipes for Beaten Doughnuts . . . Cornmeal Doughnuts . . . Orange Pecan Doughnut Balls . . . or holiday-perfect tidbits, Taffy Apple Doughnuts.

And the next time you have the neighbors in for coffee, earn admiring glances by offering them a coffee cake still warm from your oven. Think how they'll exclaim over Caramel-Pecan Coffee Cake . . . Peach Coffee Cake . . . or that all-time favorite, Streusel-filled Coffee Cake.

Why not explore this section now, and choose a recipe to prepare. You'll dazzle everyone — and only you will know how easily these home-tested recipes are prepared!

APPLE BUTTER DOUGHNUTS

2 eggs	1 tsp. soda
1 c. sugar	1/2 tsp. salt
2 tbsp. soft butter	1/2 tsp. cinnamon
1/2 c. apple butter	1/2 tsp. nutmeg
5 1/2 c. sifted all-purpose	1 tbsp. lemon juice
flour	2/3 c. evaporated milk
2 tsp. baking powder	Brown Butter Icing

Beat the eggs, sugar and butter in a large bowl with electric mixer until mixed. Beat in the apple butter. Sift flour, baking powder, soda, salt and spices together. Stir the lemon juice into evaporated milk. Add dry ingredients to egg mixture alternately with evaporated milk, beginning and ending with dry ingredients and blending well after each addition. Cover and chill for at least 2 hours. Turn onto a well-floured pastry board or cloth and knead 5 or 6 times. Roll out to about 1/4-inch thickness and cut with a floured doughnut cutter. Fry in deep fat at 375 degrees for 3 to 4 minutes or until golden, turning once. Drain on absorbent paper and cool. Frost with Brown Butter Icing. About 3 dozen.

Brown Butter Icing

1/4 c. butter	2 1/2 c. unsifted
1/4 to 1/3 c. evaporated milk	confectioners' sugar

Melt the butter in a saucepan over low heat, then cook until golden brown. Remove from heat and blend in the milk alternately with sugar until smooth and of desired spreading consistency.

BEATEN FRENCH DOUGHNUTS

1 c. water	1 c. sifted flour
1/2 tsp. salt	3 eggs
2 tbsp. butter	Confectioners' sugar

Place the water, salt and butter in a saucepan and bring to a boil. Stir until butter is melted. Add the flour and stir until smooth. Place in a large bowl and cool slightly. Beat in eggs, one at a time, then beat for 5 minutes. Cover and refrigerate for 2 hours. Place in a pastry tube and press onto flat pan dusted with flour to the size of small doughnuts. Let stand for 1 to 2 hours to dry. Fry in deep fat at 375 degrees until browned. Drain on absorbent paper and dust with confectioners' sugar.

Mrs. Becky Baker, Roseboro, North Carolina

CAKE DOUGHNUTS

4 eggs	3 tsp. baking powder
Sugar	3/4 tsp. salt
1/3 c. milk	2 tsp. cinnamon
1/3 c. melted shortening	1/2 tsp. nutmeg
3 1/2 c. sifted flour	

Beat the eggs and 2/3 cup sugar in a bowl until light. Add milk and shortening and mix well. Sift the flour, baking powder, salt, 1 teaspoon cinnamon, and nutmeg together. Add to the egg mixture and mix well. Chill thoroughly. Roll out 3/8 inch thick on a lightly floured surface and cut with floured doughnut cutter. Let stand for 15 minutes. Fry in deep fat at 375 degrees until brown, turning once. Drain on paper towels. Shake in a bag containing 1/2 cup sugar and remaining cinnamon. About 2 dozen.

Sylvia Baker, Lexington, Kentucky

SWEET CREAM GREBBLES

2 tbsp. sugar	1/4 tsp. soda
1 c. cream	3 eggs, well beaten
1 c. buttermilk	2 tsp. baking powder
1/2 tsp. salt	4 c. flour

Mix all ingredients well and refrigerate for 3 hours. Roll out as for doughnuts and cut in desired shapes. Fry in deep, hot fat until brown and roll in additional sugar while warm. 12 servings.

Mrs. James Waller, Oklahoma City, Oklahoma

COCONUT DOUGHNUTS

2 eggs	2 1/3 c. sifted flour
1/2 c. sugar	2 tsp. baking powder
1/4 c. milk	1/2 tsp. salt
2 tbsp. salad oil	1/2 c. flaked coconut

Beat the eggs with sugar in a bowl until light, then stir in the milk and oil. Sift dry ingredients together and add to the egg mixture. Add the coconut and stir until blended. Chill for several hours. Roll out on a lightly floured surface 1/2 inch thick and cut with a doughnut cutter. Fry in deep fat at 375 degrees until brown, then turn and brown on other side. Drain on paper towels and sprinkle with additional sugar. 1 dozen.

Mary Carlisle, Covington, Kentucky

CORNMEAL DOUGHNUTS

3/4 c. milk	1 1/2 c. flour
1 1/2 c. white cornmeal	2 tsp. baking powder
1/2 c. butter	1/4 tsp. cinnamon
3/4 c. sugar	1 tsp. salt
2 eggs, beaten	

Heat the milk in a saucepan. Stir in the cornmeal and cook, stirring, for 10 minutes. Remove from heat. Add the butter and sugar, then stir in the eggs. Sift the flour with baking powder, cinnamon and salt and stir into the cornmeal mixture. Roll out on a floured board and cut with a doughnut cutter. Fry in deep, hot fat until brown. Drain well and roll in additional sugar.

Mrs. Samuel T. Smith, Huntsville, Alabama

TAFFY APPLE DOUGHNUTS

2 1/4 c. flour	2 eggs, beaten
2 tsp. baking powder	1/2 c. milk
1 tsp. salt	1 tsp. vanilla
1/4 tsp. nutmeg	3/4 c. honey
1/4 c. shortening	3/4 c. brown sugar
1/2 c. sugar	Chopped nuts

Sift the flour, baking powder, salt and nutmeg together. Blend shortening and sugar in a bowl, then blend in eggs. Combine milk and vanilla and add to sugar mixture alternately with flour mixture, beating well after each addition. Drop by spoonfuls into hot, deep fat and fry for 3 to 4 minutes or until golden brown. Drain on absorbent paper and insert wooden skewer or stick in each ball. Combine the honey and brown sugar in a saucepan and bring to a boil. Dip each ball into hot honey syrup and roll in nuts. Cool. 3 1/2 dozen.

Mrs. Loraine Ricchirelli, Jacksonville, Florida

TEXAS GOLDEN PUFFS

2 c. sifted flour	1/4 c. corn oil
1/4 c. sugar	3/4 c. milk
3 tsp. baking powder	1 egg
1 tsp. salt	Cinnamon sugar
1 tsp. nutmeg or mace	

Sift the dry ingredients together into a bowl. Add the oil, milk and egg and beat until mixed. Drop by teaspoonfuls into hot fat and fry for about 3 minutes or until golden brown. Drain on absorbent paper and roll in cinnamon sugar. 2 1/2 dozen.

Opal Walker Rocke, Brownsville, Texas

POTATO DOUGHNUTS

4 c. sifted all-purpose flour	1 3/4 c. sugar
3 tsp. baking powder	1/4 c. melted shortening
2 tsp. salt	1 c. mashed potatoes
2 1/2 tsp. ground nutmeg	1 tbsp. grated lemon peel
1/4 tsp. soda	1/3 c. buttermilk
2 lge. eggs, well beaten	1 1/2 tsp. ground cinnamon

Sift the flour, baking powder, salt, nutmeg and soda together. Beat the eggs with 1 1/4 cups sugar and shortening in a bowl, then stir in potatoes and lemon peel. Add the flour mixture alternately with buttermilk. Turn out onto a lightly floured board and roll to 1/4-inch thickness. Cut with a doughnut cutter. Drop 4 or 5 doughnuts at a time into deep fat at 350 degrees. Cook until doughnuts rise to the surface, turning to brown both sides, then drain on absorbent paper. Mix remaining sugar and the cinnamon in a small bag. Add several doughnuts at a time and toss to cover with sugar mixture. Doughnuts may be coated with confectioners' sugar instead of cinnamon sugar, if desired. 36 doughnuts.

ORANGE-PECAN DOUGHNUT BALLS

2 c. sifted flour	2 tbsp. orange juice
1/2 tsp. soda	1/2 c. chopped pecans
1/4 tsp. salt	1/4 c. chopped raisins
2 egg yolks, beaten	1/4 c. chopped dates
1/2 c. sugar	1 tsp. grated orange rind
1/2 c. sour milk	

Sift the flour, soda and salt together into a bowl. Combine the egg yolks, sugar, sour milk and orange juice and stir into the flour mixture. Stir in the pecans, raisins, dates and orange rind. Drop from teaspoon into deep fat at 350 degrees and fry for 4 to 5 minutes or until brown, turning once. Drain on paper towels and roll in additional sugar. 2 dozen.

Ethel Lewis, Lafayette, Louisiana

PINEAPPLE-SOUR CREAM BRUNCH RING

1 1-lb. 4 1/2-oz. can crushed pineapple	2 c. sifted flour
2 tbsp. sliced almonds	1 tsp. soda
1 3-oz. package cream cheese	1 tsp. salt
1 c. sugar	1/2 c. sour cream
2 tsp. vanilla	1 tbsp. soft butter
1 egg	1 to 1 1/2 c. confectioners' sugar

Drain the pineapple well and reserve 1/2 cup. Grease a 9-inch tube pan or mold and sprinkle with almonds. Beat the cream cheese in a bowl until soft. Beat in the sugar and vanilla, then blend in the egg. Sift the flour with soda and salt and add to cream cheese mixture alternately with sour cream. Stir in the remaining pineapple and turn into prepared pan. Bake in 350-degree oven for 45 minutes or until coffee cake tests done. Place on a wire rack and let stand for 10 minutes. Remove from pan. Mix reserved pineapple, butter and confectioners' sugar in a bowl. Spread over warm coffee cake.

Photograph for this recipe on page 88.

CORN FLAKE COFFEE CAKE

1 1/2 c. sifted flour	1 c. sugar
1 tsp. cinnamon	2 eggs
1 tsp. baking powder	1 c. sour cream
1/2 tsp. soda	1 c. corn flake crumbs
1/2 tsp. salt	1/2 c. (packed) brown sugar
1/2 c. butter or margarine	1/2 c. finely chopped pecans

Sift the flour with cinnamon, baking powder, soda and salt. Cream the butter in a bowl. Add sugar and cream well. Add the eggs and beat well. Add dry ingredients alternately with sour cream, then stir in 1/2 cup corn flake crumbs. Combine remaining corn flake crumbs, brown sugar and pecans. Pour 1/2 of the batter into a greased 9 x 9 x 2-inch pan and sprinkle with 1/2 of the pecan mixture. Add remaining batter and sprinkle with remaining pecan mixture. Bake at 350 degrees for 40 minutes or until done. Cut into squares to serve.

Mrs. Novella Shoaf, Hickory, North Carolina

PINEAPPLE BUTTERCRUMB COFFEE CAKE

1 1-lb. 4 1/2-oz. can	1 egg
pineapple tidbits	2 c. sifted flour
1/2 c. soft butter	2 1/2 tsp. baking powder
1/2 c. sugar	1 tsp. salt
1/8 tsp. almond extract	1/2 c. milk
1/2 tsp. vanilla	Cinnamon-Butter Crumbs

Drain the pineapple well and reserve 1/2 cup tidbits. Blend the butter with sugar and flavorings in a bowl until light, then beat in the egg. Sift the flour with baking powder and salt and add to sugar mixture alternately with milk. Stir in remaining pineapple tidbits. Turn into a greased and floured 9 x 9 x 2-inch pan or 1 1/2-quart mold and place reserved pineapple tidbits on top. Cover with Cinnamon-Butter Crumbs. Bake in 350-degree oven for 45 to 50 minutes or until coffee cake tests done. Serve warm. 8 servings.

Cinnamon-Butter Crumbs

1/2 c. sifted flour	1/4 tsp. cinnamon
1/2 c. sugar	1/4 c. butter

Combine all ingredients in a bowl and blend well.

CARAMEL-PECAN COFFEE CAKE

3/4 c. (packed) brown sugar	3/4 c. shortening
1/3 c. chopped pecans	1 egg
1/4 c. melted butter	1 3/4 c. flour
1 tbsp. light corn syrup	3/4 c. milk
3/4 c. sugar	

Combine the brown sugar, pecans, butter and corn syrup and mix well. Spread in bottom of a greased 8-inch square pan. Cream the sugar, shortening and egg thoroughly in a bowl and add flour alternately with milk, stirring just until all flour is moistened. Spread over pecan mixture. Bake at 375 degrees for 35 to 40 minutes.

Nina Humphrey, Burkesville, Kentucky

CINNAMON-BUTTERMILK COFFEE CAKE

2 1/3 c. sifted flour	1 c. buttermilk
2 c. (firmly packed) light	1 tsp. soda
brown sugar	1 tsp. cinnamon
1/2 c. butter or margarine	1/2 c. chopped nuts
1 egg, beaten	

Preheat oven to 350 degrees. Mix 2 cups flour and brown sugar in a bowl and cut in the butter until mixture resembles coarse meal. Reserve 3/4 cup for topping. Add remaining flour to remaining butter mixture and mix well. Add the egg, buttermilk, soda and cinnamon and mix just until dry ingredients are moistened. Pour into a greased 9-inch square pan. Mix reserved butter mixture and nuts and sprinkle over mixture in pan. Bake for 50 to 55 minutes, then cool. 9 servings.

Frances Gordon, Danielsville, Georgia

HARD-TO-BEAT COFFEE CAKE

1 c. butter	2 tsp. soda
2 3/4 c. sugar	1 pt. sour cream
4 eggs	2 tsp. vanilla
3 c. flour	3 tsp. cinnamon
2 1/2 tsp. baking powder	1 c. chopped nuts

Cream the butter and 2 cups sugar in a bowl, then add the eggs, one at a time, beating well after each addition. Sift the flour, baking powder and soda together and add to creamed mixture alternately with the sour cream. Add vanilla and mix well. Mix the cinnamon, nuts and remaining sugar. Place 1/2 of the batter in a greased 9 x 13-inch pan and sprinkle with half the cinnamon mixture. Add remaining batter and sprinkle with remaining cinnamon mixture. Bake at 350 degrees for 45 to 50 minutes. Cool on wire rack.

Mrs. Elroy W. Smith, Charleston, South Carolina

PEACH COFFEE CAKE

1 egg	3 tbsp. salad oil
1 c. sugar	1/2 tsp. vanilla
1 c. all-purpose flour	2 c. sliced peaches
1 tsp. baking powder	2 tbsp. raisins
1/2 tsp. salt	1/2 tsp. cinnamon
1/4 c. milk	

Beat the egg in a bowl until light. Add 1/2 cup sugar gradually and beat well. Sift the flour, baking powder and salt together. Combine the milk, oil and vanilla and add to egg mixture alternately with flour mixture. Place in a greased 8-inch square pan. Arrange peach slices on top and sprinkle with raisins. Mix remaining sugar and cinnamon and sprinkle over raisins. Bake at 350 degrees for 30 to 40 minutes. Serve warm.

Mrs. W. A. Hughes, Starkville, Mississippi

SCONES WITH MARMALADE

4 c. all-purpose flour	1/4 c. margarine
1 tsp. soda	Buttermilk
1 tsp. cream of tartar	Orange marmalade
1/2 tsp. salt	

Sift the flour, soda, cream of tartar and salt together into a bowl and cut in the margarine. Stir in enough buttermilk to make a stiff dough. Knead on a floured surface until smooth. Roll out half the dough at a time to a circle 1 inch thick, then cut into wedges. Place on a greased baking sheet. Bake at 400 degrees for 15 minutes or until brown. Serve with marmalade.

HONEY COFFEE CAKE

1 1/2 c. sifted flour	3 tbsp. melted shortening
1/2 c. sugar	1 9-oz. can crushed
2 tsp. baking powder	pineapple, drained
3/4 tsp. salt	1/4 c. butter or margarine
1 egg, beaten	1/3 c. honey
1/2 c. milk	1/4 c. shredded coconut

Sift dry ingredients together into a bowl. Combine the egg, milk and shortening and add to dry ingredients. Mix just until smooth. Pour into a greased 8 x 8 x 2-inch baking pan and cover with pineapple. Cream the butter and honey in a bowl and spoon over pineapple. Sprinkle with coconut. Bake in 400-degree oven for about 30 minutes or until done.

Mrs. Dan Parker, Prescott, Arizona

FRUIT AND ALMOND COFFEE CAKE

1 c. mixed candied fruits	1 tsp. soda
1/2 c. chopped almonds	1 tsp. salt
Sifted all-purpose flour	1/2 c. butter
1 1/4 c. sugar	1 tsp. almond extract
1 tsp. cinnamon	2 eggs
1 tsp. baking powder	1 c. sour cream

Chop the candied fruits and place in a small mixing bowl. Add the almonds and 1 tablespoon flour and toss until fruits and almonds are coated. Blend 1/4 cup sugar with the cinnamon. Sift 2 cups flour, baking powder, soda and salt together. Cream the butter, remaining sugar and almond extract in a large bowl until light and fluffy. Add the eggs, one at a time, beating well after each addition. Stir in the flour mixture alternately with sour cream, beginning and ending with flour mixture. Pour half the batter into a greased 8-inch tube pan. Sprinkle with half the fruit mixture, then sprinkle with half the cinnamon mixture. Repeat layers. Swirl a knife through the batter several times with a twisting motion. Bake in a 350-degree oven for about 50 minutes or until a cake tester inserted in center comes out clean. Cool in the pan on a wire rack, then remove from pan.

Bea Evans, Clearwater, Florida

QUICK COFFEE CAKE

1 c. flour	1/2 c. milk
3 tsp. baking powder	4 tbsp. melted butter or
1/2 c. sugar	margarine
Dash of salt	1/2 c. cinnamon sugar
1 egg, beaten	

Sift the flour, baking powder, sugar and salt together into a bowl. Mix the egg, milk and butter. Add to flour mixture and mix well. Turn into a greased 8 x 8-

inch pan and sprinkle with cinnamon sugar. Bake at 400 degrees for 15 minutes or until brown.

Mrs. Harry Kuehner, Deerfield Beach, Florida

FRUIT BREAD

1/2 c. seedless raisins	4 eggs
1/2 c. currants	1/4 c. citron
1 c. butter or margarine	3 tbsp. brandy
1 c. sugar	1 1/2 c. flour
Grated rind of 1/2 lemon	1/2 tsp. baking powder
Dash of nutmeg	Fine bread crumbs

Place the raisins and currants in a bowl and cover with hot water. Let stand for about 30 minutes. Drain, then place on absorbent paper. Cream the butter in a bowl. Add the sugar gradually and mix well. Stir in the grated rind and nutmeg. Add the eggs, one at a time, beating well after each addition. Stir in the raisins, currants, citron and brandy. Sift the flour with baking powder into the butter mixture and mix well. Sprinkle enough bread crumbs into a greased loaf pan to coat sides and bottom. Pour the raisin mixture into the pan. Bake at 325 degrees for 1 hour and 30 minutes or until bread tests done. Remove from pan and cool. Wrap in aluminum foil and store for 4 to 5 days before slicing.

SOUR CREAM-PECAN COFFEE CAKE

2 c. sifted cake flour	1 tsp. vanilla
1 tsp. baking powder	2 eggs
1 tsp. soda	1 c. sour cream
1/4 tsp. salt	1 tbsp. cinnamon
1/2 c. butter	1/4 c. chopped pecans
1 1/4 c. sugar	

Sift the flour with baking powder, soda and salt. Cream the butter, 1 cup sugar and vanilla thoroughly in a large bowl, then beat in the eggs, one at a time. Add the flour mixture alternately with sour cream, beating until smooth after each addition. Pour 1/2 of the batter into a greased and floured tube pan. Combine remaining sugar, cinnamon and pecans and sprinkle 1/2 of the mixture over batter. Add remaining batter, then sprinkle with remaining pecan mixture. Bake at 350 degrees for 40 minutes or until done. 6-8 servings.

Marilyn Truitt, Charleston, South Carolina

SPICY COFFEE CAKE

1/2 c. butter or margarine	1/4 tsp. salt
1 1/3 c. sugar	1 1/2 tsp. baking powder
2 eggs, beaten	1 tsp. vanilla
1 tsp. soda	1/2 c. chopped nuts
1 c. sour cream	1 tsp. cinnamon
1 1/2 c. flour	

Cream the butter in a bowl, then beat in 1 cup sugar gradually. Add the eggs and mix well. Mix the soda and sour cream and stir into butter mixture. Sift the flour, salt and baking powder together and add to sour cream mixture gradually. Add vanilla and mix well. Mix the nuts, remaining sugar and cinnamon and sprinkle 2 tablespoons in a greased and floured tube pan. Add half the batter. Sprinkle with remaining nut mixture and pour remaining batter on top. Bake at 350 degrees for 45 minutes. Invert onto a plate and remove pan. Cool. Sprinkle with powdered sugar, if desired.

Mrs. Yolanda T. Bota, Springfield, Georgia

STREUSEL-FILLED COFFEE CAKE

3/4 c. sugar	1 1/2 c. sifted flour
1/4 c. soft shortening	2 tsp. baking powder
1 egg	1/2 tsp. salt
1/2 c. milk	

Mix the sugar, shortening and egg in a bowl and stir in milk. Sift dry ingredients together and stir into sugar mixture. Spread half the batter in a greased and floured 9-inch square pan.

Streusel

1/2 c. (packed) brown sugar
2 tbsp. flour
2 tsp. cinnamon

2 tbsp. melted butter
1/2 c. chopped nuts

Mix all ingredients well and sprinkle half the mixture on batter in pan. Add remaining batter and sprinkle nut mixture over top. Bake at 375 degrees for 30 to 35 minutes.

Mrs. Julian Green, Gainesville, Florida

SAFFRON COFFEE RING

1 c. margarine
1/2 c. sugar
2 eggs
1/2 c. chopped raisins
1 1/4 c. milk

1/2 tsp. saffron
3 1/4 c. sifted flour
4 tsp. baking powder
1/4 c. chopped almonds

Mix the margarine with sugar in a bowl. Add 1 egg, raisins and milk and mix. Dissolve the saffron in 1 tablespoon hot water, then stir into the egg mixture. Add the flour and baking powder and mix well. Shape into a roll. Place on a greased baking sheet and shape into a ring. Beat remaining egg and brush on ring. Sprinkle with the almonds and additional sugar. Bake in 450-degree oven for 10 to 15 minutes.

pancakes
& waffles

Few quick breads are so versatile as pancakes and waffles. They brighten up a dull breakfast . . . add excitement to a luncheon or tea . . . and make unusual desserts for dinner or supper. Coupled with all this versatility is good flavor — these popular breads take on delicious taste when served with syrups and fruit, or dressed up with whipped cream or sauces.

Creative cooks from Maryland to Texas have turned their impressive talents toward developing pancake and waffle recipes which make the most of this flavor excitement — and the results are well worth eating, as the recipes in this section demonstrate!

Are pancakes among your family's favorite foods? Then experiment with Banana Pancakes . . . Cornmeal Hot Cakes . . . or such dessert pancakes as Crepes and Peaches or Crepes Suzette. Why not serve pancakes in new guise — Potato Pancakes are just perfect with a pot roast or served in traditional German style, with sauerbraten. And don't forget the waffles. American families love them.

These and other great home-style recipes are yours in the pages that follow. Carefully developed until any error has been cooked out, these recipes offer you a chance to serve your family's favorite foods in new dress — and to earn compliments in the process!

STRAWBERRY ROLL-UPS

1 pt. fresh strawberries	1/2 pt. sour cream
Sugar	1/2 tsp. soda
1/2 c. soft margarine	1/4 c. flour
4 eggs	3 tbsp. melted margarine

Wash and clean the strawberries, then slice. Mash 3/4 cup strawberries with a fork and set aside. Place remaining strawberries in a bowl and sprinkle with 1/3 cup sugar. Cover and chill. Place the soft margarine in a small mixing bowl and beat with electric mixer until fluffy, adding 1/2 cup sugar gradually. Add the mashed strawberries, small amount at a time, beating well after each addition. Beat at high speed until light and fluffy, then chill. Beat the eggs in a bowl. Mix the sour cream with the soda, then stir into the eggs. Add the flour and melted margarine and mix well. Drop by tablespoonfuls onto a hot griddle and cook until brown, turning once. Place about 2 tablespoons sliced strawberries down center of each pancake. Roll up and place on a platter. Sprinkle with any remaining strawberry syrup. Spread fluffy strawberry topping over pancakes. 8 servings.

Photograph for this recipe on page 102.

BANANA PANCAKES

2 ripe bananas, mashed	2 c. self-rising flour
1 1/2 c. buttermilk	1/4 tsp. soda
2 eggs	2 tbsp. melted butter or
2 tbsp. sugar	salad oil

Mix the bananas, buttermilk, eggs and sugar in a bowl and beat well. Add flour and soda and beat thoroughly. Stir in the butter. Drop by spoonfuls onto a greased, hot griddle and cook until brown on both sides, turning once. Serve with butter and powdered sugar, if desired. About 1 dozen.

Eleanor Fulford, Tampa, Florida

ROLLED PANCAKES WITH ORANGE SAUCE

1 6-oz. can frozen Florida orange juice concentrate, thawed	1/4 tsp. salt
	1/4 c. flour
	3/4 c. cottage cheese
3/4 c. maple syrup	12 slices prosciutto or boiled
3 eggs, separated	ham

Combine the undiluted orange juice concentrate with maple syrup in a saucepan and heat until warm, if desired. Beat the egg whites until stiff but not dry. Beat the egg yolks in a bowl until lemon-colored. Stir in the salt, flour and cottage cheese, then fold in the egg whites. Drop by spoonfuls onto a hot, lightly greased griddle to make 12 pancakes 4 inches in diameter. Cook until golden brown on both sides, turning once. Place slice of prosciutto on each pancake and roll while warm. Place on a platter and serve with orange sauce.

BLUEBERRY-BUTTERMILK PANCAKES

2 c. sifted flour	2 eggs, beaten
1/2 tsp. salt	2 c. buttermilk
1 tbsp. baking powder	2 tbsp. melted butter
3 tbsp. sugar	2 c. blueberries

Sift 1 3/4 cups flour, salt, baking powder and sugar together. Mix the eggs, buttermilk and butter in a bowl. Add dry ingredients all at once and mix well. Toss blueberries with remaining flour and stir into batter. Pour 1/4 cup batter for each pancake onto a greased, hot griddle and cook until brown on both sides, turning once.

Mrs. R. L. Marcheasseau, Miami, Florida

CREPES SUZETTE

1 c. milk	Butter
1/2 c. water	Sugar
1 c. flour	1 tbsp. confectioners' sugar
1 egg	Juice of 1 orange
1/2 tsp. salt	3/4 to 1 c. orange liqueur
1/2 tbsp. salad oil	1 tbsp. grated orange peel
Cognac	1 tsp. grated lemon peel

Add the milk and water to flour in a bowl and beat until smooth. Add the egg, salt, salad oil and 1/2 tablespoon cognac and beat well. Refrigerate overnight. Melt just enough butter in small frying pan to cover bottom of pan and pour in 1 tablespoon batter for each crepe. Cook until honey-colored on both sides, turning crepe gently with spatula. Stack the crepes, sprinkling sugar lightly between each. Melt 1/4 cup butter in chafing dish over high heat. Add the confectioners' sugar and orange juice and cook until sugar is dissolved. Add the orange liqueur, orange peel and lemon peel and bring to a boil. Place 1 crepe in chafing dish, turn over and fold twice. Slide over to edge of dish, then repeat with remaining crepes. Add 3/4 cup cognac to liquid in dish and bring to a boil. Ignite. Ladle flaming mixture over crepes until the flame is gone. Serve crepes on warm plates with remaining liquid. 6-8 servings.

Mrs. Nicole Auzabee, Montgomery, Alabama

BUTTERMILK PANCAKES

2 c. sifted flour
1 tsp. soda
1 tsp. salt
2 tbsp. sugar

2 eggs, slightly beaten
2 c. buttermilk
2 tbsp. melted butter

Sift the flour, soda, salt and sugar into a bowl. Add the eggs, buttermilk and butter and stir just until flour is moistened. Mixture will be lumpy. Pour 1/4 cup batter for each pancake onto a hot, greased griddle and cook until bubbles cover surface. Turn and brown on other side. Serve with butter and syrup.

Mrs. Charles Bayles, Silver City, New Mexico

CREPES AND PEACHES

1/2 c. sifted flour
2 eggs
1 1/2 tbsp. sugar
3/4 c. milk
Dash of salt

1/2 tsp. vanilla
1 1-lb. can sliced peaches,
   drained
Sauce

Combine the flour, eggs, sugar, milk, salt and vanilla in a bowl and beat with an electric mixer until smooth. Refrigerate for several hours. Heat a heavy 6-inch skillet until a drop of water dances on the surface. Grease lightly and pour in 2 tablespoons batter. Lift skillet and tilt from side to side until batter covers bottom evenly. Cook until lightly browned. Repeat with remaining batter. Roll up crepes and place in a chafing dish or skillet with peach slices. Pour Sauce over all and heat through. Keep warm. 5 servings.

Sauce

1/3 c. sugar
1 tbsp. cornstarch
Dash of salt

1 1/4 c. orange juice
2 tbsp. butter
1 tsp. grated orange rind

Mix the sugar, cornstarch and salt in a bowl and blend in 1/4 cup orange juice. Bring remaining orange juice to a boil and stir in sugar mixture. Cook, stirring, until clear, then remove from heat. Add the butter and orange rind and stir until butter is melted. Serve over crepes.

Mrs. Shirley Thompson, Winston-Salem, North Carolina

LACY-EDGED CORN CAKES

1 c. white cornmeal
1/2 tsp. salt
1/2 tsp. soda
1 egg
1 1/4 c. buttermilk

Shortening
1 c. (packed) dark brown sugar
1/4 c. water
1 tbsp. butter

Mix the cornmeal, salt and soda in a bowl. Add egg and mix well. Stir in the buttermilk slowly. Heat 1 tablespoon shortening in a 12-inch skillet. Drop batter by tablespoonfuls into shortening and cook until brown on both sides, turning once and adding shortening as needed. Mix remaining ingredients in a small saucepan and bring to a boil. Cook, stirring occasionally, for 2 to 3 minutes or until the consistency of maple syrup. Serve with pancakes.

Mrs. John R. Richards, Lookout Mountain, Tennessee

ORANGE CHEESE-FILLED PANCAKES

1 8-oz. package cream cheese	2 c. sifted flour
1/2 c. sour cream	2 tsp. baking powder
2 tbsp. frozen Florida orange	2 tbsp. sugar
juice concentrate, thawed	2 eggs
3/4 tsp. salt	2 c. sour milk
1/4 c. diced green pepper	1 tsp. soda
1/4 c. diced red pepper	6 tbsp. melted shortening

Blend the cream cheese, sour cream, undiluted orange juice concentrate and 1/4 teaspoon salt in a bowl, then fold in green and red peppers. Sift the flour, baking powder, remaining salt and sugar together. Beat eggs well in a bowl. Combine the sour milk and soda. Add to eggs and mix well. Stir in the shortening. Add flour mixture and mix well. Drop by spoonfuls onto a hot griddle to make 8 pancakes, 6 inches in diameter. Cook until brown on both sides, turning once. Keep warm. Spread orange filling generously between pancakes in stacks of 4 high. Slice stacks into quarters and serve immediately.

CORNMEAL HOT CAKES

1 c. flour	1 1/2 c. boiling water
2 c. cornmeal	2 eggs
1 1/2 tsp. salt	1 3/4 c. milk
3 tsp. baking powder	3 tbsp. melted shortening

Mix the flour, half the cornmeal, salt and baking powder. Stir boiling water into remaining cornmeal in a bowl. Add the eggs and beat well. Add milk, flour mixture and shortening and mix well. Drop by spoonfuls onto a hot, greased griddle and cook until brown on both sides, turning once.

Mrs. Raymond Bryan, Delhi, Louisiana

CREAM PANCAKES

2 eggs, slightly beaten	1 1/2 tsp. sugar
1 c. light cream	1/4 tsp. salt
1/2 c. sifted flour	Sweetened strawberries

Mix the eggs and light cream in a bowl. Sift the flour, sugar, and salt together into the egg mixture and beat with a rotary beater until smooth. Refrigerate for at least 2 hours. Heat a griddle until a drop of water dances on surface, then grease lightly. Beat batter. Pour 2 tablespoons batter for each pancake on griddle and brown on both sides. Roll or fold pancakes and keep warm. Unroll and fill with strawberries just before serving, then reroll. 1 dozen.

Mrs. V. A. Collins, Big Spring, Texas

DESSERT PANCAKES

3 eggs	1/2 tsp. salt
1 1/4 c. milk	Melted butter
3/4 c. sifted flour	Strawberry Sauce
1 tbsp. sugar	

Beat the eggs in a bowl until thick and lemon-colored, then stir in milk. Sift dry ingredients together. Add to egg mixture and mix until smooth. Drop 1 tablespoon batter for each pancake on a moderately hot, greased griddle and cook until brown. Turn and brown on other side. Keep warm. Spoon melted butter over cakes and sprinkle with additional sugar. Serve with Strawberry Sauce. 3 1/2 dozen.

Strawberry Sauce

4 c. sliced strawberries	1 c. sugar
1/2 c. water	

Mix all ingredients in a saucepan and bring to a boil. Reduce heat and simmer for 10 minutes. Remove from heat and cool slightly.

Mrs. D. G. Page, Lawton, Oklahoma

GRITS PANCAKES

2 c. self-rising flour	2 tbsp. cooking oil
1 tsp. baking powder	2 eggs, beaten
1/2 c. cool cooked grits	Milk
2 tbsp. sugar	

Mix all ingredients except milk in a bowl. Stir in enough milk to make a thin batter. Pour 1 tablespoon batter for each pancake in a greased, hot skillet and cook until brown on both sides. Serve with butter and syrup, if desired.

Mrs. O. R. Anderson, Orangeburg, South Carolina

PANCAKES DELUXE

2 c. sifted flour	1/2 c. light cream
5 tsp. baking powder	2 c. milk
1/2 tsp. salt	2 eggs, beaten
2 tsp. sugar	Blueberry Sauce
1/4 c. melted butter	Sour cream

Sift the flour, baking powder, salt and sugar together. Mix the butter, cream, milk and eggs in a bowl. Add the flour mixture and beat until smooth. Drop by spoonfuls onto a lightly greased griddle and cook until brown on both sides, turning once. Spread 2 tablespoons Blueberry Sauce over center of each pancake. Roll the pancakes and place on a warm plate. Top with sour cream.

Blueberry Sauce

1/2 c. sugar	1 can blueberries
2 tsp. cornstarch	1 tbsp. lemon juice
Dash of salt	1 tsp. grated lemon rind

Combine the sugar, cornstarch, salt and blueberries in a saucepan. Bring to a boil, then reduce heat. Simmer for 4 to 5 minutes or until clear and thickened. Remove from heat and stir in lemon juice and grated rind.

ONION PANCAKES

1/3 c. minced onion	1 tbsp. sugar
2 tbsp. salad oil	1/2 tsp. salt
1 1/4 c. sifted flour	1 egg, beaten
3 tsp. baking powder	1 c. milk

Cook the onion in 1 tablespoon salad oil until tender but not brown. Sift dry ingredients together into a bowl. Combine remaining oil, the egg and milk. Add to dry ingredients and stir just until flour is moistened. Batter will be lumpy. Add the onion and mix. Drop by spoonfuls on a hot, greased griddle and cook until brown on both sides. About eight 4-inch pancakes.

Berniece Moore, Myrtle Beach, South Carolina

POTATO PANCAKES

4 med. potatoes	1/4 tsp. salt
1 sm. onion	1/8 tsp. pepper
1 egg	Shortening
2 tbsp. flour	

Grate the potatoes and drain well. Grate the onion. Combine the onion and potatoes in a bowl and mix well. Stir in the egg, then the flour, salt and pepper. Heat a small amount of shortening in a skillet over medium heat. Place 1 tablespoon potato mixture in skillet and flatten. Cook until brown. Turn and brown other side. Repeat with remaining potato mixture. 8 servings.

Mrs. Charles Huffman, Richlands, North Carolina

ROYAL RICE PANCAKES

1 c. cooked rice	1 tsp. baking powder
1 c. milk	1/2 tsp. salt
2 eggs, separated	1 tbsp. melted shortening
1 c. flour	

Mix the rice, milk and beaten egg yolks in a bowl. Sift the flour with baking powder and salt and stir into the rice mixture. Stir in the shortening, then fold in stiffly beaten egg whites. Drop by spoonfuls onto a hot, greased griddle and cook until bubbles cover surface. Turn and brown on other side.

Mrs. Henry Sherrer, Bay City, Texas

CORNMEAL-BACON WAFFLES

1 c. cornmeal	2 eggs, beaten
3/4 c. flour	1/4 c. melted butter
3 tsp. baking powder	3 strips crisply fried bacon,
Salt to taste	crumbled
1 c. milk	

Sift the cornmeal, flour, baking powder and salt together into a bowl. Stir in the milk, eggs and butter. Add bacon and mix. Bake in hot waffle iron until brown.

Mrs. E. E. McHenry, Cumberland, Virginia

CREAMED COD ON WAFFLES

6 tbsp. butter or margarine	3/4 c. Florida grapefruit juice
1/2 c. chopped onion	1/2 c. light cream
2 1/3 c. flour	3 tsp. baking powder
3 3/4 c. milk	2 tbsp. sugar
1 1/4 tsp. salt	3 eggs, separated
1/4 tsp. chervil	1/2 c. melted shortening
2 c. flaked cooked cod	

Melt the butter in a heavy saucepan over low heat. Add the onion and cook for about 3 minutes, stirring frequently. Add 1/3 cup flour slowly and stir until smooth. Stir in 2 cups milk slowly. Sprinkle with 1/2 teaspoon salt and chervil and bring to a simmer, stirring constantly. Do not boil. Add the cod and grapefruit juice and cook until cod is heated through. Remove from heat and stir in the cream. Keep warm. Sift remaining flour with baking powder, remaining salt and sugar. Beat the egg whites until stiff. Beat egg yolks in a bowl and stir in remaining milk and shortening. Add the flour mixture and beat with a rotary beater until smooth. Fold in egg whites. Pour 1/2 cup batter for each waffle into a hot waffle iron. Bake until golden brown. Serve with creamed cod.

BUTTERMILK WAFFLES

1 c. cornmeal	1 c. flour
1 1/2 c. water	3/4 tsp. soda
1 tsp. salt	1/2 c. milk
1 tbsp. shortening	1/2 c. buttermilk
2 eggs, separated	

Mix the cornmeal, water, salt and shortening in a saucepan and cook for 10 minutes, stirring constantly. Cool. Beat the egg yolks until light and stir into cornmeal mush. Sift the flour and soda together and add to mush alternately with the milk. Stir in the buttermilk and fold in stiffly beaten egg whites. Bake in a hot waffle iron until brown.

Mrs. Edna Williams, Jacksonville, Alabama

CHOCOLATE WAFFLES

6 tbsp. cocoa	2 eggs, well beaten
1/2 c. sugar	1 c. light cream
1 1/4 c. sifted cake flour	1/4 c. melted butter
1/2 tsp. salt	2 egg whites, stiffly beaten
3 tsp. baking powder	1/4 tsp. vanilla

Sift dry ingredients together into a bowl. Add the eggs and cream and mix well. Add the butter and fold in egg whites and vanilla. Bake in a hot waffle iron until brown. Three 10-inch waffles.

Hilda Madison, Parkersburg, West Virginia

CORNMEAL-SOUR MILK WAFFLES

2 c. cornmeal	2 c. sifted flour
3 c. water	1 tsp. soda
2 tsp. salt	1 c. milk
2 tbsp. butter	1 1/4 c. (about) sour milk
4 eggs	

Mix the cornmeal, water, salt and butter in top of a double boiler. Place over boiling water and cook for 10 minutes, stirring frequently. Cool. Beat the eggs until light and stir into cornmeal mixture. Sift flour with soda and add to cornmeal mixture alternately with milk. Add enough sour milk to make a thin batter. Bake in hot waffle iron until brown. 12 waffles.

Mrs. Louise Harden, Springfield, Tennessee

CORNMEAL WAFFLES

3/4 c. cornmeal	1/2 tsp. salt
1/4 c. flour	2 tsp. baking powder

1 tbsp. sugar   1/2 c. milk
1 egg, separated   4 tbsp. melted butter

Sift dry ingredients together 3 times. Beat the egg yolk in a bowl and stir in the milk and butter. Add dry ingredients and mix well. Fold in stiffly beaten egg white. Bake in hot waffle iron until brown.

Mrs. Glen Brockton, Fort Howard, Maryland

DATE DESSERT WAFFLES

2 c. sifted flour   1 3/4 c. milk
3 tsp. baking powder   1/2 c. salad oil
1 tsp. salt   2 eggs, separated
1/4 c. (packed) brown sugar   1 c. chopped dates

Sift the flour, baking powder and salt together into a bowl and stir in the brown sugar. Mix the milk, oil and beaten egg yolks and stir into flour mixture. Fold in the stiffly beaten egg whites and dates. Bake in hot waffle iron until brown. 3 large waffles.

Mrs. Roy Holland, Fort Knox, Kentucky

EASY WAFFLES

1 3/4 c. sifted flour   2 eggs, separated
3 tsp. baking powder   1 1/4 c. milk
1/2 tsp. salt   1/2 c. salad oil

Sift dry ingredients together into a bowl. Combine the beaten egg yolks and milk and stir into dry ingredients. Stir in the oil. Fold in the stiffly beaten egg whites. Bake in hot waffle iron until brown. About 8 waffles.

Mrs. S. T. Scott, Hattiesburg, Mississippi

SOUR CREAM WAFFLES

1 c. sifted flour   1 egg, separated
1/2 tbsp. sugar   1 c. sour cream
1 tsp. baking powder   1/4 c. milk
1/4 tsp. soda   3 tbsp. melted butter
1/4 tsp. salt

Sift dry ingredients together into a bowl. Combine the beaten egg yolk, sour cream, milk and butter. Add to flour mixture and beat until smooth. Fold in stiffly beaten egg white. Bake in a hot waffle iron until brown. 4 servings.

Mrs. Daisy Gilbert, Newport, Arkansas

BUTTERMILK WAFFLES

1 c. sifted flour	**5 tbsp. butter**
1/2 tsp. soda	**2 eggs, separated**
1 1/2 tsp. baking powder	**1 c. buttermilk**
1/2 tsp. salt	

Sift dry ingredients together into a bowl and cut in the butter until mixture resembles coarse meal. Beat the egg yolks well and add buttermilk. Add to flour mixture and mix just until flour is dampened. Fold in the stiffly beaten egg whites. Bake in a hot waffle baker until steaming stops. 4 waffles.

Honey Butter

1/2 c. butter	**1/2 c. honey**

Cream the butter thoroughly. Beat in the honey gradually until mixture is light and fluffy.

SOUR MILK WAFFLES

3 eggs, beaten	**2 c. flour**
2 c. sour milk	**2 tsp. salt**
1 tsp. soda	**6 tbsp. bacon drippings**

Mix the eggs and sour milk in a bowl. Sift dry ingredients together and add to egg mixture. Add the bacon drippings and mix well. Pour 3/4 cup batter into hot waffle iron and cook until brown. Repeat with remaining batter. Serve with melted butter, peanut butter and syrup. 10 waffles.

Mrs. T. D. Gault, Jr., Gaffney, South Carolina

SOUTH CAROLINA BUTTERMILK WAFFLES

1 c. flour	1 tsp. sugar
1 tsp. baking powder	2 eggs, beaten
1 tsp. salt	1 c. buttermilk
1/2 tsp. soda	2 tbsp. bacon drippings

Sift the flour, baking powder, salt, soda and sugar together into a bowl. Add the eggs, buttermilk and bacon drippings and mix well. Cook in a hot waffle iron until brown.

Mrs. T. B. Canaday, Inman, South Carolina

SOUTHERN BELLE WAFFLES

2 c. all-purpose flour	3 eggs, separated
3 tsp. baking powder	1 3/4 c. milk
3/4 tsp. salt	1/2 c. salad oil
2 tbsp. sugar	

Sift the flour with baking powder, salt and sugar 3 times and place in a bowl. Beat the egg yolks and stir in the milk and oil. Pour into flour mixture and beat with a rotary beater until smooth. Fold in stiffly beaten egg whites. Pour 1/2 cup batter for each waffle into a hot waffle iron and bake until golden brown. Serve with butter and syrup or honey.

Mrs. Bill B. Lambert, Austin, Texas

SPICE WAFFLES

1/2 c. shortening	1 tsp. allspice
1 c. (packed) brown sugar	1/2 tsp. cloves
2 eggs	1/2 c. milk
1 1/2 c. sifted flour	1/2 c. chopped walnuts
2 tsp. baking powder	2 tbsp. chopped candied ginger
1/2 tsp. salt	1 c. whipping cream, whipped
1 tsp. cinnamon	

Cream the shortening and brown sugar in a bowl. Add the eggs, one at a time, beating well after each addition. Sift the flour, baking powder, salt and spices together and add to creamed mixture alternately with milk. Stir in the walnuts. Bake in a hot waffle iron until brown. Fold the candied ginger into the whipped cream and serve on waffles. 2-3 large waffles.

Sandra Reeves, Leesville, Louisiana

loaves & coffee cakes

WITH MIXES

In former times, southern women depended upon their own creativity and the recipes which had been handed down from their ancestors to create tasty loaves and coffee cakes. Today, thanks to the wonders of modern food processing, homemakers can rely on prepackaged mixes to take much of the work out of preparing their favorite breads. Yet convenience notwithstanding, creativity still is important in preparing these breads and coffee cakes.

Ingenuity is certainly reflected in the recipes you'll find in the pages that follow. Timesaving, yes, but the good flavor and fine texture that characterize southern foods are guaranteed with these home-tested recipes. Thrill your family and friends by preparing Barbecue Bread or Biscuit Skillet Bread for your next backyard cookout. Holidays? Of course your precious minutes are at a premium but at the same time you want to prepare special breads. Save time and effort with recipes for Cranberry-Orange Relish Bread . . . Candied Fruit Ring . . . or Lemon Coffee Cake. These breads practically shout "seasons greetings," and only you will know they are based on prepackaged mixes!

For easy preparation and fabulous flavor, you'll certainly come to depend on the following compilation of family-approved recipes for loaves and coffee cakes using mixes!

117

HONEY-ALMOND-CRANBERRY BREAD

2 c. fresh cranberries	2 eggs, well beaten
6 c. biscuit mix	1 c. honey
1 tsp. ground allspice	1/2 c. milk
Grated rind of 1 orange	1/2 c. orange juice
1 c. chopped blanched almonds	

Rinse and drain the cranberries and place in a bowl. Add the biscuit mix, allspice, orange rind and almonds and mix. Add the eggs, honey, milk and orange juice and beat until well blended. Spoon into 2 greased and floured 9 x 5 x 3-inch loaf pans. Bake in 350-degree oven for 50 to 55 minutes or until top springs back when touched. Unmold and cool thoroughly on a rack. Slice thinly to make sandwiches with fillings of cream cheese and jelly, deviled ham and thinly sliced apple or peanut butter and sliced bananas.

APRICOT-NUT BREAD

3/4 c. (firmly packed) brown sugar	1 egg, slightly beaten
3/4 c. chopped pecans	1 1/4 c. orange juice
1 c. chopped dried apricots	3 c. packaged biscuit mix

Combine the sugar, pecans and apricots in a bowl and stir in the egg and orange juice. Add the biscuit mix and beat for about 30 seconds. Turn into a greased 9 x 5-inch loaf pan. Bake at 350 degrees for 45 minutes or until toothpick inserted in center comes out clean.

Mrs. R. M. Denver, San Antonio, Texas

118

BANANA-DATE LOAF

3/4 c. mashed ripe bananas	1 pkg. date muffin mix
1/3 c. water	

Mix the bananas and water. Prepare the muffin mix according to package directions, using banana mixture instead of the water. Pour into a greased loaf pan. Bake at 350 degrees for 45 to 55 minutes or until done. Remove from pan and cool. Let set for 1 day before slicing.

Mrs. C. B. Washington, Tulsa, Oklahoma

BANANA-NUT BREAD

1 c. sugar	1 c. crushed ripe bananas
1/4 c. shortening	2 c. packaged biscuit mix
2 eggs, slightly beaten	1/4 c. chopped nuts

Cream the sugar and shortening in a bowl. Add the eggs, bananas, biscuit mix and nuts and beat until well mixed. Pour into a well-greased loaf pan. Bake in 350-degree oven for 1 hour. Remove from pan and cool on rack before slicing.

Mrs. L. J. Kelley, Charleston, South Carolina

BARBECUE BREAD

1 egg, well beaten	1 1/2 c. packaged biscuit mix
1/2 c. milk	2 tbsp. grated Parmesan cheese
3 tbsp. onion soup mix	1 tbsp. sesame seed
1/2 c. grated Cheddar cheese	2 tbsp. melted margarine

Combine the egg and milk. Add the soup mix and Cheddar cheese to biscuit mix in a bowl. Add milk mixture and stir just until dry ingredients are moistened. Place in a greased loaf pan. Sprinkle with Parmesan cheese and sesame seed and drizzle butter over top. Bake at 400 degrees for 25 minutes.

Hilda Smith, Raleigh, North Carolina

BISCUIT SKILLET BREAD

1 can mushroom soup	2 c. packaged biscuit mix
2 eggs, beaten	1/4 c. butter or margarine
2 tbsp. salad oil	1/4 c. grated Parmesan cheese
1 tsp. instant minced onion	

Mix the soup, eggs and oil. Stir the onion into biscuit mix in a bowl and make a well in the center. Pour in the soup mixture and blend. Melt the butter in a large iron skillet. Spoon batter into the skillet and sprinkle with cheese. Bake at 400 degrees for 25 minutes. 6-8 servings.

Mrs. James A. Fleming, Ocala, Florida

BLUEBERRY SUPPER BREAD

1 pkg. blueberry muffin mix	**1/4 c. flour**
1/2 c. sugar	**2 tbsp. butter or margarine**

Prepare the muffin mix according to package directions for coffee cake and pour into a greased 8 1/2-inch round baking dish. Combine the sugar and flour in a bowl and cut in butter until mixture is consistency of crumbs. Sprinkle on blueberry mixture in baking dish. Bake in 400-degree oven for 30 minutes or until done. Serve warm with butter. 6-8 servings.

Ellen Brent, Chester, South Carolina

BOSTON BROWN BREAD

1 pkg. gingerbread mix	**1 c. seedless raisins**
3/4 c. yellow cornmeal	**1 1/4 c. water**
3/4 c. flour	

Combine all ingredients in a large mixing bowl and mix well. Pour into a greased 9 x 5-inch loaf pan. Bake at 375 degrees for 35 to 40 minutes, then remove from pan immediately. Serve warm or cold.

Joan Becker, Port Arthur, Texas

CARDAMOM BRAID

1 pkg. hot roll mix	**1/2 c. golden seedless raisins**
2 tbsp. melted margarine	**Milk**
1 tsp. crushed cardamom	**Sugar**

Prepare the hot roll mix according to package directions. Add the margarine, cardamom and raisins and mix well. Cover and let rise in a warm place until doubled in bulk. Knead on a lightly floured surface for about 1 minute, then divide in thirds. Roll each third with hands to form a strand 10 inches long and taper ends. Place 1 inch apart on a greased baking sheet. Braid the strands loosely, beginning in the middle and working toward either end, then pinch ends together. Cover and let rise for 40 minutes or until doubled in bulk. Brush with milk and sprinkle with sugar. Bake in 375-degree oven for about 25 minutes or until done. Serve hot.

Mrs. O. A. Burke, Staunton, Virginia

CORN BREAD WHEEL

1 pkg. corn muffin mix	**1 can luncheon meat, cut in**
3/4 c. grated sharp cheese	**strips**
2 tbsp. minced green pepper	

Prepare the muffin mix according to package directions and stir in the cheese and green pepper. Grease a skillet and arrange luncheon meat in a wheel pattern on bottom of skillet. Pour the batter over luncheon meat strips. Bake at 375 degrees for 30 to 35 minutes or until done. Invert on a plate to serve.

Mrs. Thelma Hoopaugh, Hiram, Georgia

CORNY CORN BREAD

1 12-oz. package corn muffin mix	1/2 tsp. dry mustard
1 12-oz. can whole kernel corn with sweet peppers	1 sm. onion, chopped
	1 egg, beaten
	2/3 c. milk

Combine the muffin mix, corn, mustard and onion in a bowl. Add the egg and milk and blend well. Spread in a greased skillet. Bake at 400 degrees for 20 minutes or until brown. 9 servings.

Mrs. Fran Stone, Clarendon, Arkansas

CRUNCHY CORN BREAD

1 12-oz. package corn muffin mix	3/4 c. salted peanuts
2/3 c. milk	3 tbsp. grated Parmesan cheese
1 egg, slightly beaten	Paprika

Combine the muffin mix, milk and egg in a bowl and pour into a greased jelly roll pan. Sprinkle peanuts over top and press into batter. Sprinkle with cheese. Bake at 400 degrees for 15 to 20 minutes or until golden brown, then sprinkle with paprika. Cut into squares. 20 servings.

Rosalind Casey, Newport, Kentucky

GARLIC CORN BREAD

1 8-oz. package corn muffin mix	1/2 c. grated Parmesan cheese
1 c. chopped salted peanuts	1 tsp. garlic salt
	3 tbsp. melted margarine

Prepare the muffin mix according to package directions and spread in a well-greased jelly roll pan. Sprinkle with peanuts, cheese and garlic salt and drizzle butter over top. Bake at 375 degrees for about 25 minutes or until lightly browned. Cut into squares and cool slightly. Remove from pan and serve warm.

Mrs. Martin J. Clark, Wilmington, Delaware

GREEN CHILIES CORN BREAD

1/3 c. canned green chilies	2 tbsp. bacon drippings
1 pkg. corn bread mix	1 c. shredded sharp American process cheese
1 9-oz. can cream-style corn	

Drain, rinse and seed the green chilies. Cut in strips and drain on paper towels. Prepare the corn bread mix according to package directions and stir in the corn and bacon drippings. Spoon half the batter into a greased 9 x 9 x 2-inch pan. Place chilies over batter and sprinkle with half the cheese. Cover with remaining batter, then add remaining cheese. Bake according to package directions.

Eleanor Vickers, Jackson, Mississippi

MISSISSIPPI CORN BREAD

1/4 lb. sliced bacon	2 tbsp. sugar
3 c. corn bread mix	1 onion, minced
3 eggs	1 c. cream-style corn
2 1/2 c. milk	1/4 c. chopped pimento
1/2 c. grated cheese	Chopped hot peppers to taste

Fry the bacon until crisp. Drain and crumble. Combine remaining ingredients in order listed and stir in the bacon. Pour into a greased 13 x 9 1/2 x 2-inch baking dish. Bake at 425 degrees until brown. 15 servings.

Mrs. Frank McCollum, Birmingham, Alabama

ONION BREAD

1/2 c. chopped onion	1/2 c. sour cream
2 tbsp. butter or margarine	1/2 c. shredded sharp American
1 pkg. corn muffin mix	process cheese

Cook the onion in butter until tender but not brown. Prepare the muffin mix according to package directions. Pour into a greased 8 x 8 x 2-inch baking pan and sprinkle with onion. Mix the sour cream and cheese and spoon over onion. Bake in 400-degree oven for 25 minutes or until done. Cut into squares.

Joellen Lenox, Pendleton, West Virginia

TOPPER CORN BREAD

1/4 c. chopped onion	1 c. shredded sharp American
1 tbsp. butter or margarine	process cheese
1 pkg. corn bread mix	1 tsp. celery seed

Cook the onion in butter until tender but not brown. Prepare the corn bread mix according to package directions and place in a greased 10 x 6 x 1/2-inch baking dish. Sprinkle cheese over top. Sprinkle onion over cheese, then sprinkle with celery seed. Bake at 375 degrees for 20 minutes or until done. Serve at once. 8 servings.

Virginia T. Bond, Madison, West Virginia

CORN BREAD DELUXE

1 8-oz. package corn	1 c. whole kernel corn, drained
bread mix	3 tbsp. melted shortening

Prepare the corn bread mix according to package directions. Add the corn and mix well. Melt the shortening in a skillet and pour corn bread mixture into the skillet. Bake at 400 degrees for 30 minutes or until brown. Serve hot. 4-6 servings.

Mrs. J. A. Brown, Cascade, Maryland

CRAZY QUILT BREAD

1/2 c. sugar	3 c. packaged biscuit mix
1 egg	1/2 c. mixed candied fruits
1 1/4 c. milk	3/4 c. chopped nuts

Preheat oven to 350 degrees. Mix the sugar, egg, milk and biscuit mix and beat vigorously for 30 seconds. Batter will be lumpy. Blend in the fruits and nuts and pour into a well-greased 9 x 5 x 3-inch loaf pan. Bake for 45 minutes or until toothpick inserted in center comes out clean. Cool before slicing.

Mrs. Eleanor Malloy, Meridian, Mississippi

DATE BREAD

1/2 c. hot water	1 tsp. baking powder
1 14-oz. package date bar mix	1 c. mashed bananas
3 eggs, slightly beaten	3/4 c. chopped walnuts
1/4 c. sifted flour	

Mix the hot water and date filling portion of the mix in a bowl. Add crumbly portion of mix, eggs, flour, baking powder and bananas and beat for 2 minutes. Stir in the walnuts and pour into a greased 9 1/2 x 5 x 3-inch loaf pan. Bake in a 350-degree oven for 50 to 55 minutes or until done. Remove from pan and cool.

Mrs. R. L. Painter, Mountain View, Arkansas

LEMON BREAD

1 box lemon cake mix	4 eggs
1 3 3/4-oz. package instant	1/2 c. salad oil
lemon pudding mix	1 c. cold water
1/2 2-oz. box poppy seed	

Mix the cake mix, pudding mix and poppy seed in a bowl. Add the eggs, oil and water and beat well. Pour into 2 greased and floured 9 x 5-inch loaf pans. Bake at 350 degrees for 45 to 55 minutes.

Billie Butler, Brunswick, Georgia

NUT BREAD

1 c. sugar	1/2 c. chopped nuts
1 egg	2 c. packaged biscuit mix
1 c. milk	

Combine all ingredients in a bowl and mix well. Pour into a greased loaf pan. Bake at 350 degrees for 1 hour.

Anna Cooper, Russellville, Alabama

HERB LOAF

1 pkg. hot roll mix
1 tsp. sage

1/2 tsp. crushed basil

Reserve 1/4 cup hot roll mix. Prepare remaining hot roll mix according to package directions. Add the sage and basil to reserved mix and sprinkle on a flat surface. Add the roll mixture and knead for 2 to 3 minutes or until smooth. Place in a greased bowl and turn to grease top. Cover and let rise in a warm place for 1 hour or until doubled in bulk. Punch down. Shape into a ball and place in a greased 9-inch pie plate. Let rise for about 40 minutes. Bake in 375-degree oven for 35 to 40 minutes or until done. Remove from plate and brush with butter, if desired.

Marilyn Greene, Donaldsonville, Louisiana

ONION-CHEESE BREAD

1/2 c. chopped onion
1 egg, beaten
1/2 c. milk
1 1/2 c. packaged biscuit mix

1 c. shredded sharp American
   process cheese
2 tbsp. parsley flakes
2 tbsp. melted butter

Cook the onion in small amount of hot fat until tender but not brown. Combine the egg and milk. Add to biscuit mix in a bowl and stir until just mixed. Add the onion, half the cheese and parsley and mix. Place in a greased 8-inch round cake pan. Sprinkle with remaining cheese and drizzle butter over top. Bake at 400 degrees for 20 minutes or until toothpick inserted in center comes out clean. 6-8 servings.

Mrs. Susan T. Campana, West Hollywood, Florida

SMALL CRANBERRY-ORANGE LOAVES

1 pkg. orange muffin mix
1 c. whole cranberry sauce

1 c. chopped pecans

Prepare the muffin mix according to package directions. Mash the cranberry sauce and stir into the muffin mixture. Add pecans and mix. Pour into well-greased 12-ounce juice cans, filling 2/3 full. Place on a cookie sheet. Bake at 350 degrees for 30 minutes or until golden brown. Cool and remove from cans.

Mrs. Edith Pollock, Kerens, Texas

RAISIN LOAF

1 pkg. hot roll mix
1/2 c. seedless raisins
1 c. powdered sugar

1 to 1 1/2 tbsp. milk
1/4 tsp. vanilla

Prepare the hot roll mix according to package directions, adding raisins with the egg. Cover and let rise in a warm place for about 45 minutes or until doubled in bulk. Place in a greased 8 1/2 x 4 1/2 x 2 1/2-inch loaf pan. Cover and let rise for 45 minutes or until doubled in bulk. Bake in 375-degree oven for 45 to 50 minutes or until done. Cool for 10 minutes, then remove from pan. Cool. Combine the powdered sugar, milk and vanilla and mix until smooth. Spread on loaf.

Mrs. Roger Estes, Wilcox, Arizona

SAVORY SUPPER BREAD

1/2 c. chopped onion
1 tbsp. shortening
1 egg, beaten
1/2 c. milk
1 1/2 c. packaged biscuit mix

1 c. grated sharp American
 process cheese
1 tbsp. poppy seed
2 tbsp. melted butter

Cook the onion in shortening until light brown. Combine the egg and milk. Add to the biscuit mix in a bowl and stir just until dry ingredients are moistened. Add the onion and half the cheese. Spread in a greased 8-inch square pan. Sprinkle with remaining cheese and poppy seed and drizzle with butter. Bake at 400 degrees for 20 to 25 minutes. Serve hot. 6-8 servings.

Mrs. Dorothy Coffee, Silver City, New Mexico

PICALILLI HOT BREAD

2 c. packaged biscuit mix
2/3 c. milk
1 egg, slightly beaten
2 tbsp. instant minced onion
1 tbsp. oil

1/3 c. drained sweet pickle
 relish
1/4 c. grated Parmesan or
 American cheese

Place the biscuit mix in a large bowl. Combine the milk, egg, onion, oil and relish. Add all at once to biscuit mix and stir until just mixed. Turn into a greased 8-inch square pan and sprinkle with cheese. Bake in 400-degree oven for 20 minutes or until done. Serve hot. 6-8 servings.

Gloria Ridgeway, Winter Haven, Florida

CRANBERRY-ORANGE RELISH BREAD

1 pkg. orange muffin mix
1 egg

1 c. cranberry-orange relish

Combine the muffin mix with egg and relish until just blended. Mixture will be lumpy. Pour into a greased loaf pan. Bake at 350 degrees for 45 minutes or until golden brown.

Betty Walton, Delaware City, Delaware

YEAST-RAISIN BREAD

1 pkg. dry yeast	4 c. packaged biscuit mix
1 1/4 c. warm water	2/3 c. raisins
2 tbsp. sugar	Shortening

Dissolve the yeast in warm water in a mixing bowl. Add the sugar and half the biscuit mix and beat for 2 minutes, scraping side and bottom of bowl frequently. Add remaining biscuit mix and raisins and blend until smooth. Cover with a cloth and let rise in a warm place for about 30 minutes or until doubled in bulk. Stir down, then place in a greased loaf pan. Let rise in a warm place for 30 to 40 minutes or until doubled in bulk. Bake at 375 degrees for 45 to 50 minutes or until browned. Remove from pan and place on a rack. Brush top with shortening and cool before slicing.

Mrs. Richard Milling, Tulsa, Oklahoma

APPLE AND WALNUT RING

1 pkg. hot roll mix	2 tsp. cinnamon
1 c. (packed) brown sugar	1/4 c. melted margarine
1 c. chopped tart apples	1/2 c. chopped walnuts
1/4 c. soft margarine	1/4 c. honey

Prepare the hot roll mix according to package directions. Let rise until doubled in bulk. Mix the brown sugar, apples, soft margarine and cinnamon and spread on bottom of 10-inch tube pan. Knead dough on a lightly floured surface until smooth and elastic. Shape into 1-inch balls. Dip in melted margarine and roll in walnuts. Place layer of balls in prepared pan and drizzle half the honey over balls. Add remaining balls and drizzle remaining honey over top. Cover and let rise in a warm place for 40 to 45 minutes or until doubled in bulk. Bake at 350

degrees for about 40 minutes or until done, then cool in pan for 10 minutes. Invert onto a plate and serve warm.

Lucy Fuller, Fayetteville, North Carolina

COFFEE-COT CAKE

1 13 3/4-oz. package hot roll mix	Dash of nutmeg
1 c. dried California apricots	2 tbsp. melted butter or margarine
1 c. sugar	1/2 c. chopped walnuts
1 c. water	1/2 c. sifted confectioners' sugar
1/4 c. (firmly packed) light brown sugar	1 tbsp. milk
Dash of cinnamon	1/8 tsp. vanilla

Prepare roll mix and let rise according to package directions. Combine the apricots, sugar and water in a saucepan and bring to a simmer, stirring constantly. Cook for 15 minutes or until apricots are soft. Drain the apricots and reserve syrup. Add enough water to reserved syrup, if necessary, to make 1 cup liquid. Puree apricots with syrup in an electric blender or force apricots through a food mill and combine with liquid. Add the brown sugar and spices and cool. Roll out dough on a lightly floured surface to 32 x 8-inch strip. Brush with some of the melted butter. Spread apricot filling on top, reserving 1/3 cup, and sprinkle with walnuts. Roll dough from long side as for jelly roll and pinch edges to seal. Spiral the roll of dough, seam side down, in a greased 8-inch springform pan, starting at center of pan, then brush remaining butter over top. Cover with a towel and let rise in a warm place for about 45 minutes or until doubled in bulk. Bake in 350-degree oven for 50 minutes. Cool for 10 minutes, then remove from pan. Place on a rack. Blend reserved apricot filling with 1 tablespoon water and spread over coffee cake. Mix remaining ingredients and drizzle over coffee cake, if desired. Serve warm.

Photograph for this recipe on page 116.

FROSTED POLKA-DOT COFFEE CAKE

1/4 c. warm water	1 egg, well beaten
1 pkg. yeast	2 3/4 c. biscuit mix
1/2 c. sugar	2/3 c. jam
1/2 c. lukewarm mashed potatoes	1/3 c. confectioners' sugar
1/4 c. softened margarine	1 tsp. hot water
1/2 tsp. cinnamon	1/2 tsp. vanilla
1/4 tsp. salt	

Pour the warm water into a large, warm bowl. Add the yeast and stir until dissolved. Add the sugar, potatoes, margarine, cinnamon, salt and egg and blend well. Add half the biscuit mix and mix. Add remaining biscuit mix and mix well. Press into a greased 9-inch square pan. Cover and let rise in a warm place, free from draft, for 45 minutes or until doubled in bulk. Make depressions with handle of a wooden spoon at 1 to 2-inch intervals and fill depressions with jam. Bake in 400-degree oven for about 20 minutes or until done. Cool slightly. Mix the confectioners' sugar, hot water and vanilla and drizzle over coffee cake. Marmalade or preserves may be substituted for jam.

CANDIED FRUIT RING

1 pkg. hot roll mix	1 c. powdered sugar
1/2 c. candied fruits and peels	1 to 1 1/2 tbsp. milk
1/2 c. broken walnuts	1/4 tsp. vanilla
1/4 c. seedless raisins	

Prepare the hot roll mix according to package directions, adding the candied fruits and peels, walnuts and raisins. Let rise for about 1 hour or until doubled in bulk. Divide in half and roll each half into a rope about 24 inches long. Place on a greased baking sheet. Twist the ropes together and shape into a ring. Cover and let rise until doubled in bulk. Bake at 375 degrees for 20 to 25 minutes or until done, then cool. Mix the powdered sugar, milk and vanilla until smooth and spread on the coffee cake. Garnish with additional candied fruits and peels.

Cordelia Hughes, Beaufort, South Carolina

LEMON COFFEE CAKE

4 c. packaged biscuit mix	1 egg, beaten
3/4 c. (packed) brown sugar	6 tbsp. melted butter
1 tsp. cinnamon	1 tsp. grated lemon peel
1/4 tsp. nutmeg	1/4 c. chopped walnuts
1 1/4 c. milk	

Combine the biscuit mix, 1/4 cup brown sugar, and spices in a bowl and mix well. Combine the milk, egg and 1/4 cup butter. Add to dry ingredients and beat for 30 seconds. Mix remaining brown sugar, lemon peel and walnuts. Pour half the batter into a greased 9 x 9-inch baking pan. Drizzle with 1 tablespoon butter and sprinkle with half the walnut mixture. Repeat layers. Bake in 350-degree oven for about 35 minutes or until done. Serve warm.

Mrs. L. L. Deas, Harlan, Kentucky

CINNAMON CRESCENTS

1 pkg. hot roll mix	1 c. chopped walnuts
4 eggs	1 c. sugar
1/2 c. soft butter or margarine	2 tbsp. cinnamon
2 c. seedless raisins	

Dissolve the yeast from hot roll mix in a large bowl according to package directions. Beat 3 eggs well and add to the yeast. Add the roll mix and butter and blend thoroughly. Cover and let rise in a warm place until doubled in bulk. Knead on a floured board until smooth. Divide in half and roll each half to 15 x 12-inch rectangle. Beat remaining egg lightly and brush on dough. Combine remaining ingredients and sprinkle half over each rectangle. Roll each as for jelly roll, starting with 15-inch side, and place, seam side down, on a greased baking sheet. Curve to form crescents and pinch ends to seal. Cover and let rise for 30 minutes. Bake in 375-degree oven for 20 to 25 minutes or until done. Frost with confectioners' icing, if desired.

Mrs. Faye Kelley, Silver Spring, Maryland

JOLLY BREAKFAST RING

2/3 c. milk	12 cherries
2 c. packaged biscuit mix	1/2 c. chopped nuts
5 tbsp. melted butter	1/2 c. sugar
3 tbsp. brown sugar	1 tsp. cinnamon

Mix the milk and biscuit mix in a bowl and shape into 12 balls. Pour 3 tablespoons butter into a 9-inch ring mold and sprinkle with brown sugar. Place the cherries on the brown sugar and add 1/4 cup nuts. Roll balls in remaining butter, then in mixture of sugar, cinnamon and remaining nuts. Place in ring mold. Bake in 400-degree oven for 30 minutes. Remove from pan. 8 servings.

Mrs. M. A. Samford, Millington, Tennessee

DUTCH APPLE COFFEE CAKE

1 13-oz. package coffee cake mix	1 No. 2 can apple pie filling
	1/4 c. sugar
2 tbsp. melted butter	1 tsp. cinnamon
1 egg, beaten	1/2 c. chopped pecans

Mix the coffee cake mix according to package directions, using 1 cup water. Stir in the butter and egg. Let rise in a warm place for about 1 hour or until doubled in bulk. Spoon into a greased 13 x 9 x 2-inch baking pan and spoon apple pie filling over batter. Mix the sugar and cinnamon and sprinkle over pie filling. Top with the pecans. Cover and let rise in a warm place for 30 to 40 minutes or until doubled in bulk. Bake in a 400-degree oven for 20 to 25 minutes. Drizzle with powdered sugar icing, if desired. Hot roll mix may be substituted for the coffee cake mix.

BLUEBERRY COFFEE CAKE

2 c. biscuit mix	1 1/2 c. fresh blueberries
1 c. sugar	2 tbsp. soft butter or
1/2 c. instant nonfat dry milk	margarine
2/3 c. water	1/4 c. all-purpose flour
1 egg	

Preheat oven to 350 degrees. Place the biscuit mix, 2/3 cup sugar and 1/4 cup dry milk in a 3-quart bowl. Add the water and egg and beat well with mixer at medium speed. Pour into a greased and floured 9-inch pan and cover with blueberries. Mix remaining sugar, butter, remaining dry milk and flour and sprinkle over blueberries. Bake for about 50 minutes or until cake pulls away from side of pan. Frozen blueberries, thawed and drained, may be substituted for fresh blueberries.

CINNAMON COFFEE CAKE

1 egg	1 c. pancake mix
Sugar	3 tbsp. melted shortening
1/2 c. milk	1/2 tsp. cinnamon

Beat the egg in a bowl until light and fluffy, then add 1/2 cup sugar, small amount at a time. Stir in the milk, pancake mix and shortening. Pour into a greased 8-inch square pan and sprinkle 2 tablespoons sugar and cinnamon on top. Bake in 400-degree oven for 20 minutes. 4-6 servings.

Mrs. Leon Purdy, West Point, Virginia

130

ORANGE COFFEE CAKE

1/2 pkg. orange muffin mix	3 tbsp. flour
2 tbsp. pineapple preserves	2 tbsp. butter or margarine
3 tbsp. sugar	3 tbsp. chopped walnuts

Prepare the muffin mix according to package directions and pour into a greased 8-inch round pan. Spread preserves over batter. Combine the sugar and flour in a bowl and cut in the butter until mixture is consistency of crumbs. Stir in the walnuts and sprinkle over batter. Bake at 400 degrees for 18 to 20 minutes or until done. Serve warm.

Mrs. Parker Curtis, Wheeling, West Virginia

STREUSEL COFFEE CAKE

1 pkg. yellow cake mix	1 1/2 c. sour cream
1/4 c. butter	1 c. sifted confectioners' sugar
1 c. (packed) brown sugar	1 to 2 tbsp. warm water
3/4 c. chopped pecans	1/2 tsp. vanilla
3 eggs	

Place 2/3 cup cake mix in a small bowl and cut in butter. Stir in the brown sugar and pecans and set aside. Beat the eggs lightly in a bowl and stir in the sour cream. Blend in remaining cake mix until just mixed. Pour half the batter into a greased and floured 13 x 9 x 2-inch pan and sprinkle half the brown sugar mixture over batter. Spoon remaining batter into pan and top with remaining brown sugar mixture. Bake at 350 degrees for 40 to 45 minutes. Mix the confectioners' sugar, water and vanilla in a bowl, then spread over warm coffee cake.

Barbara Jones, Union City, Tennessee

SWEET PETALS COFFEE CAKE

1 pkg. hot roll mix	1/2 c. melted butter or
3/4 c. sugar	margarine
1/4 c. (packed) brown sugar	1/2 c. powdered sugar
2 tsp. cinnamon	1 to 2 tsp. milk
3/4 c. chopped nuts	

Cut a 12 1/2-inch circle of aluminum foil and place on a cookie sheet. Turn up outside edge 1/2 inch, then grease the foil. Mix the hot roll mix according to package directions and let rise until doubled in bulk. Pinch off pieces of dough and roll into 6-inch round strips about 1/2 inch thick. Combine the sugar, brown sugar, cinnamon and nuts. Dip the strips into melted butter, then into sugar mixture. Wind 1 strip into pinwheel design, beginning at center of foil. Continue the pinwheel design, adding remaining strips until all are used. Cover and let rise until doubled in bulk. Bake at 350 degrees for 25 to 30 minutes. Combine the powdered sugar and milk and drizzle over the coffee cake. Serve warm. Pull petals apart to serve. 8 servings.

Mrs. Rosalind Evans, El Paso, Texas

muffins, biscuits & rolls

WITH MIXES

Every homemaker would love to serve her family freshly-baked muffins, biscuits, and rolls — but often there is not the time to prepare these treats from scratch! Now, you can assure yourself of just-perfect breads in a minimum of time when you use any of today's prepackaged mixes and the recipes you'll find in this section.

Every one of these recipes is the dependable personal favorite of a southern woman who has served it over and over again to her family and friends. There's nothing ordinary-tasting about these recipes — they all reflect the loving care that has gone into their development and perfection.

At your next supper or dinner, highlight the main course with one of these easy-to-prepare recipes. Just imagine how impressed your family will be when you carry in Maryland Beaten Biscuits, a quick and easy version of one of the South's most treasured recipes. You might want to serve Corned Beef Roll-ups, Cheese Bread Sticks, Crescent Rolls, or even homemade Onion Hamburger Buns. The recipes for these and other timesaving muffins, biscuits, and rolls are yours in the section that follows.

Save yourself time and still earn precious compliments by serving one of these tried and proven favorites at your next meal!

CRISPY CORN STICKS

1/2 c. finely chopped onion
2 tbsp. melted butter or
   margarine
1 14-oz. package corn muffin
   mix

1 12-oz. can vacuum-pack
   golden whole kernel corn,
   drained
Oil
Corn syrup

Saute the onion in butter in a saucepan until tender. Prepare muffin mix according to package directions, stirring in onion and corn with dry ingredients. Do not overmix. Brush corn stick pan liberally with oil and fill pan so batter is level with top. Keep remaining batter refrigerated until baked. Bake at 400 degrees for about 20 minutes. Remove sticks from pan and brush tops with corn syrup. 21 corn sticks.

BANANA CORN BREAD MUFFINS

1 15-oz. package corn bread
   mix
1/2 c. sugar
1/4 tsp. baking powder

3 med. bananas, mashed
1/4 c. lukewarm water
1 egg

Combine the corn bread mix, sugar and baking powder in a mixing bowl. Add the bananas, water and egg and beat for 1 minute. Spoon into fluted paper liners placed in large muffin cups. Bake at 425 degrees for 15 to 20 minutes. 12 large muffins.

Mrs. Charles R. Owen, Memphis, Tennessee

CHEESE-CORN MUFFINS

1 8-oz. package corn muffin
   mix
1 egg, beaten
1 8-oz. can cream-style corn

1/2 c. shredded sharp American
   process cheese
1/8 tsp. hot sauce

Combine all ingredients in a bowl and mix well. Fill well-greased 2 1/2-inch muffin cups 2/3 full. Bake in 425-degree oven for 15 to 20 minutes or until done. 12 muffins.

Mrs. E. N. Franklin, Lynchburg, Virginia

CINNAMON-BANANA MUFFINS

2 c. packaged biscuit mix
2 1/4 tsp. cinnamon
Sugar
1 egg, beaten

1 c. milk
1/4 c. vegetable oil
3 bananas, mashed

Mix the biscuit mix, 2 teaspoons cinnamon and 1/3 cup sugar in a bowl. Add the egg, milk and oil and mix. Add the bananas and stir until blended. Batter will be lumpy. Fill lined or greased muffin tins 3/4 full. Combine remaining cinnamon and 1 tablespoon sugar and sprinkle over muffins. Bake in 425-degree oven for 20 minutes. 18 muffins.

Mrs. Richard L. Moore, Lubbock, Texas

APPLESAUCE PUFFS

1/2 c. sugar
1 1/4 tsp. cinnamon
2 c. packaged biscuit mix
1/2 c. applesauce

1/4 c. milk
1 egg, slightly beaten
2 tbsp. salad oil
2 tbsp. melted butter

Mix 1/4 cup sugar and 1/4 teaspoon cinnamon and reserve. Combine the biscuit mix and remaining sugar and cinnamon in a bowl. Add the applesauce, milk, egg and salad oil and beat vigorously for 30 seconds. Fill greased muffin cups 2/3 full. Bake at 400 degrees for 12 minutes or until done. Cool slightly and remove from pan. Dip tops of muffins in melted butter, then in reserved sugar mixture. 12 large muffins.

Nancy Finch, Fort Sill, Oklahoma

FRENCH BREAKFAST PUFFS

2 c. packaged biscuit mix	3/4 c. milk
3/4 c. sugar	1 egg
1/4 tsp. nutmeg	1/2 c. melted butter
2 tbsp. soft butter or	1 tsp. cinnamon
shortening	

Combine the biscuit mix, 1/4 cup sugar, nutmeg, soft butter, milk and egg in a bowl and beat vigorously for 30 seconds. Fill greased muffin cups 2/3 full. Bake at 400 degrees for 15 minutes or until done. Roll in melted butter, then in mixture of remaining sugar and cinnamon. Serve hot. 12 medium muffins.

Mrs. Richard McPherson, Asheville, North Carolina

PIMENTO-CHEESE SWIRLS

1 pkg. hot roll mix	2 tbsp. chopped pimento
1 egg, slightly beaten	2 c. grated sharp American
1/2 tsp. salt	process cheese
1/2 tsp. celery seed	Dash of pepper

Prepare the hot roll mix and let rise according to package directions. Combine remaining ingredients. Divide dough into 2 parts and roll each part to a 12 x 9-inch rectangle on a lightly floured surface. Spread the cheese mixture on rectangles. Roll each rectangle as for jelly roll, starting at long side, and seal edges. Cut in 1-inch slices and place, cut side down, in well-greased 2 3/4-inch muffin cups. Cover and let rise until almost doubled in bulk. Bake at 400 degrees for 15 minutes or until done. 2 dozen.

Mrs. Vance Langley, Sumter, South Carolina

PINWHEEL MUFFINS

2 c. packaged biscuit mix	1 c. (packed) brown sugar
2/3 c. milk	2 tsp. cinnamon
4 tbsp. melted butter or margarine	

Prepare the biscuit mix with milk according to package directions for rolled biscuits and knead on a floured board for several minutes. Roll out into rectangle 1/4 inch thick and spread with butter. Sprinkle with 3/4 cup brown sugar and cinnamon. Grease a muffin pan and sprinkle remaining brown sugar in the cups. Roll dough as for jelly roll and cut into 12 slices. Place, cut side down, in muffin cups on brown sugar. Bake at 400 degrees for 10 to 15 minutes. Turn out of pan immediately and serve hot. 12 muffins.

Alice Nixon, Parkersburg, West Virginia

POLKA DOT MUFFINS

1 c. fresh cranberries, chopped	1/2 c. orange juice
3/4 c. sugar	2 tbsp. salad oil
1 tsp. grated orange peel	2 c. packaged biscuit mix
1 egg, beaten	

Combine the cranberries, 1/2 cup sugar and orange peel and set aside. Combine the egg, remaining sugar, orange juice and salad oil. Add all at once to the biscuit mix in a bowl and stir until dry ingredients are moistened. Fold in cranberry mixture, then fill greased muffin cups 2/3 full. Bake in 400-degree oven for 25 minutes or until done. 1 dozen.

Brenda Miller, Princeton, West Virginia

BLUEBERRY BISCUIT SCHNITT

2 c. fresh blueberries	1 tbsp. cornstarch
2 c. biscuit mix	2 tsp. grated orange rind
2/3 c. milk	1 egg, beaten
2 tbsp. sugar	

Rinse and drain the blueberries. Mix the biscuit mix and milk in a bowl and stir until well mixed. Knead on a lightly floured board until smooth. Roll out to an 8 x 16-inch rectangle and place the blueberries in a mound down center of length of the rectangle. Mix the sugar with cornstarch and orange rind and sprinkle over blueberries. Fold over top and bottom of the rectangle 1 inch to enclose the ends of the filling. Fold 1 side of the dough over the filling and fold remaining side over dough. Place the roll, seam side down, on a greased cookie sheet and brush with the egg. Bake at 400 degrees for 20 to 25 minutes. Remove from cookie sheet with a spatula and place on a rack. Cool and cut into 1-inch slices.

APPLE BISCUITS

1 c. crushed bite-sized
   shredded wheat biscuits
1/2 c. grated apples
1/2 c. apple juice

2 c. packaged biscuit mix
1/8 tsp. nutmeg
1/8 tsp. cinnamon

Preheat oven to 450 degrees. Mix the shredded wheat crumbs and apples in a bowl and add the apple juice. Add remaining ingredients and mix thoroughly. Drop by spoonfuls onto buttered cookie sheet. Bake for 10 minutes. 16-18 biscuits.

Mrs. F. L. Burns, Rockville, Maryland

BACON BARS

1/2 c. shredded sharp American
   process cheese
6 slices crisp bacon, crumbled

2 c. packaged biscuit mix
3 tbsp. bacon drippings

Add the cheese and bacon to the biscuit mix, then prepare according to package directions, substituting bacon drippings for salad oil. Knead on a floured surface and roll to 10 x 6-inch rectangle. Cut in six 10-inch strips. Cut each strip in thirds crosswise and place 1-inch apart on an ungreased baking sheet. Bake at 450 degrees for 10 minutes. 18 bars.

Mrs. Ira Moore, Winter Park, Florida

BISCUITS A LA ONION

2 c. diced onions
2 tbsp. margarine
3/4 tsp. salt
Dash of pepper

2 c. packaged biscuit mix
1 egg, beaten
1/2 c. sour cream

Brown the onions in the margarine in a saucepan and add 1/2 teaspoon salt and pepper. Prepare the biscuit mix according to package directions and press into a greased 8 x 8 x 2-inch pan. Top with onions. Mix the egg, sour cream and remaining salt and pour over onions. Bake at 450 degrees for about 20 minutes or until lightly browned. Cut in squares.

Dorothy Dennis, Newport, Kentucky

CHEESE CHIPS

1 1/4 c. pancake mix
1/2 c. cornmeal
1/3 c. shortening
2/3 c. milk

1/2 c. crushed potato chips
20 sm. cubes American process
   cheese

Mix the pancake mix and cornmeal in a bowl and cut in the shortening until mixture resembles coarse crumbs. Add the milk and stir until mixed. Shape into 20 balls, using 1 tablespoon dough for each. Roll in crushed potato chips and place on a greased cookie sheet. Place a cheese cube on each ball and press into dough. Bake at 450 degrees for 10 to 12 minutes. 18-20 biscuits.

Mrs. C. L. Devine, Marshallberg, North Carolina

CORNED BEEF ROLL-UPS

1 env. onion soup mix	3/4 c. cream
2 c. water	1 15-oz. can corned beef hash
2 c. packaged biscuit mix	1/4 tsp. pepper

Mix the soup mix and water in a 9-inch square baking pan and bring to a boil. Remove from heat. Mix the biscuit mix and cream in a bowl. Turn out on a lightly floured board and knead 8 times. Roll out to 12 x 8-inch rectangle. Spread corned beef hash over dough and sprinkle with pepper. Roll as for jelly roll. Cut in 1 1/2-inch thick slices with a sharp knife and place in pan containing hot soup, cut side down. Bake at 450 degrees for 30 minutes. 4 servings.

Myrtle Moss, Chattanooga, Tennessee

EASY BREAD STICKS

6 tbsp. butter or margarine	1 tbsp. sugar
2 c. packaged biscuit mix	1/2 c. milk

Melt the butter in a 13 x 9 x 2-inch baking pan. Combine the biscuit mix, sugar and milk in a mixing bowl and stir until mixed. Beat vigorously for 20 strokes. Turn out on a board lightly dusted with additional biscuit mix and knead 10 times. Roll out to a 12 x 8-inch rectangle and cut in half lengthwise. Cut each half crosswise into 16 strips. Dip each strip in melted butter in the pan, turning to coat both sides, and arrange in 2 rows in the pan. Bake in 400-degree oven for about 12 minutes or until golden brown. Serve warm. 32 bread sticks.

Mrs. Floyd Craig, Nolan, Texas

MARYLAND BEATEN BISCUITS

2 c. packaged biscuit mix	1/2 c. ice water

Combine the biscuit mix and ice water in a bowl and mix well. Place on a floured board and knead for 15 minutes. Roll out 1/2 inch thick and cut with a 1 1/2-inch biscuit cutter. Prick with a fork and place on an ungreased baking sheet. Bake at 450 degrees for 15 minutes. 2 dozen.

Mrs. Fern Coffield, Salem, Kentucky

OVEN-BUTTERED CORN STICKS

4 tbsp. butter or margarine	1 8 3/4-oz. can cream-style
2 c. packaged biscuit mix	corn

Melt the butter in a 15 1/2 x 10 1/2-inch baking pan. Combine the biscuit mix and corn in a bowl and stir until mixed. Knead 15 times on a lightly floured board. Roll out to 6 x 10-inch rectangle and cut into 1 x 3-inch strips. Roll in butter in the pan, then arrange in pan in single layer. Bake at 450 degrees for 10 to 12 minutes. 20 sticks.

Judy L. Revell, Marianna, Florida

SESAME SEED-CHEESE BISCUITS

1 c. packaged biscuit mix	1/3 c. half and half
1/4 c. shredded Cheddar cheese	1 tbsp. melted butter
1 tbsp. toasted sesame seed	

Combine the biscuit mix, cheese, sesame seed and half and half in a bowl and mix well. Shape into balls and place on a greased baking sheet. Brush with butter. Bake at 450 degrees for 10 to 15 minutes or until lightly browned.

Mrs. Lamar Jackson, Gordon, Georgia

SWEET POTATO BISCUITS

2 c. packaged biscuit mix	2 tbsp. sugar
2 tbsp. shortening	1 pkg. instant sweet potatoes

Prepare the biscuit mix according to package directions, adding the shortening and sugar. Prepare instant sweet potatoes according to package directions and stir into the biscuit mixture. Knead on a floured surface, then cut with a biscuit cutter. Place on a greased cookie sheet. Bake at 450 degrees for 10 to 12 minutes.

Mrs. Douglas Lynum, Columbus, Mississippi

APPLE PINWHEEL ROLLS

2 c. packaged biscuit mix	1/2 c. sugar
1 pkg. dry yeast	2 tbsp. butter
3/4 c. lukewarm milk	Red food coloring
1 c. chopped apples	1/2 c. boiling water
1/2 tsp. cinnamon	

Mix the biscuit mix, yeast and milk in a bowl and let rise until doubled in bulk. Roll out on a floured surface to a rectangle 1/4 inch thick. Spread with apples and roll as for jelly roll. Cut in 1-inch slices and place slices, cut side down, in a greased baking pan. Let rise until doubled in bulk. Mix the cinnamon, sugar, butter, desired amount of food coloring and boiling water and pour over rolls in pan. Bake at 375 degrees for 35 to 40 minutes. 4-5 servings.

Shirley Adams, Conway, Arkansas

CRESCENT ROLLS

1 pkg. dry yeast	2 1/2 c. packaged biscuit mix
3/4 c. warm water	Melted butter

Dissolve the yeast in water in a bowl. Add the biscuit mix and beat vigorously. Turn out onto a floured surface and knead until smooth. Roll out to a 12-inch circle and cut into 16 wedges. Roll each wedge from wide side to point and place on a greased cookie sheet, point side down. Cover with a cloth and let rise for about 1 hour or until doubled in bulk. Bake at 400 degrees for 10 to 15 minutes or until golden brown. Brush with butter.

Esther Lake, Chandler, Arizona

CHERRY BREAKFAST ROLLS

1 1-lb. jar red maraschino cherries	2 tbsp. melted butter or margarine
1 13 3/4-oz. package hot roll mix	1/2 c. currant jelly

Drain the cherries and cut in halves. Prepare the roll mix and let rise according to package directions. Roll out on a lightly floured surface to 1/4-inch thickness and cut into 24 squares. Brush with the butter. Combine the cherries and jelly and mix well. Place some of the cherry mixture on each rectangle. Overlap 2 opposite corners of each square and pinch together. Place on greased baking sheets and let rise in a warm place for 40 to 50 minutes or until doubled in bulk. Bake in 375-degree oven for 20 to 25 minutes or until brown. 2 dozen.

CHEESE BREAD STICKS

1 pkg. hot roll mix	1 tbsp. poppy seed
1 c. shredded sharp American	1/4 c. melted butter or
process cheese	margarine

Prepare the hot roll mix according to package directions, adding cheese and poppy seed. Let rise until doubled in bulk, then divide in half. Roll out each half on a lightly floured surface to a 10 x 6-inch rectangle and cut in twenty 6-inch long strips. Roll each strip between hands until shape of a pencil. Place on a greased baking sheet and brush with melted butter. Let rise for 30 to 45 minutes or until doubled in bulk. Bake in 400-degree oven for 10 minutes or until done. 40 sticks.

Mrs. John P. Kilpatrick, Lake Charles, Louisiana

CARAMEL ROLL-UPS

1 pkg. hot roll mix	1 c. golden brown sugar
1/2 c. sour cream	1/2 c. raisins

Prepare hot roll mix and let rise according to package directions. Knead on a lightly floured board for 5 minutes. Roll out into a 15 x 10-inch rectangle. Spread sour cream over the dough and sprinkle with brown sugar and raisins. Roll from long side as for jelly roll and seal seam. Cut in 1-inch slices and place, cut side up, in a greased 9-inch baking pan. Do not crowd. Place any remaining slices in greased muffin cups. Let rise in a warm place for about 30 minutes or until almost doubled in bulk. Bake at 375 degrees for 20 to 25 minutes or until done. Serve warm. 12-15 rolls.

Photograph for this recipe on page 132.

BABAS WITH PEACH COBBLER SAUCE

1 13 3/4-oz. package hot roll mix	1 tbsp. sugar
1/4 c. warm water	1 egg, beaten
1/2 c. warm milk	Peach Cobbler Sauce
	Sweetened whipped cream

Dissolve the yeast from package of hot roll mix in warm water in a bowl, then stir in the milk, sugar and egg. Add remainder of package of hot roll mix to yeast mixture and blend well. Cover and let rise for 30 to 45 minutes or until doubled in bulk. Place the dough in 10 well-greased 6-ounce custard cups and let rise for 30 to 45 minutes or until doubled in bulk. Bake in 400-degree oven for 15 to 20 minutes. Remove rolls from custard cups. Punch small holes in each roll with a toothpick and split each roll in half horizontally. Place halves, cut side up, in a large shallow dish and pour Peach Cobbler Sauce over rolls. Refrigerate for several hours, spooning sauce over rolls occasionally. Place halves of each roll back together in individual serving dishes and spoon some of the Peach Cobbler Sauce and whipped cream over each roll.

Peach Cobbler Sauce

1 c. water	2 7 3/4-oz. jars junior baby food peach cobbler
1/2 c. sugar	6 tbsp. dark rum
Dash of salt	

Mix the water, sugar and salt in a saucepan. Bring to a boil over medium heat, stirring constantly until sugar is dissolved. Remove from heat and stir in the peach cobbler and rum.

QUICK FRUIT BUNS

1 pkg. hot roll mix	1/3 c. sugar
2 tbsp. melted butter or margarine	1 tsp. cinnamon
2 tbsp. golden seedless raisins	1/2 tsp. nutmeg
2 tbsp. chopped candied fruits and peels	1 egg, lightly beaten
	Confectioners' icing

Prepare the hot roll mix according to package directions, adding butter, raisins, fruits and peels, sugar and spices to flour mixture and mix well. Cover with a damp cloth and let rise in a warm place for about 1 hour or until doubled in bulk. Turn out on a lightly floured surface and knead until smooth. Shape into 12 buns. Place on a lightly greased baking sheet. Cover and let rise for about 45 minutes or until almost doubled in bulk. Mix the egg and 1 tablespoon water and brush over buns. Bake at 375 degrees for about 15 minutes or until done, then cool slightly. Spread with confectioners' icing.

Mrs. S. H. King, Hampton, Virginia

HOT BREAD STICKS

1 pkg. hot roll mix   Salt
1 egg white, slightly beaten

Prepare the hot roll mix according to package directions, using 1 cup warm water and omitting the egg. Let rise until doubled in bulk. Place on a lightly floured surface and knead. Cut off pieces slightly smaller than golf balls and roll each with hands to 10-inch pencil-thin stick. Place on a greased baking sheet. Mix the egg white with 1 tablespoon water and brush on bread sticks. Let rise for about 20 minutes. Brush again with egg white mixture and sprinkle with salt. Bake at 450 degrees for about 12 minutes. 2 1/2 dozen.

Mrs. William Dillard, Dallas, Texas

ONION HAMBURGER BUNS

1 c. chopped onion   1 pkg. hot roll mix
2 tbsp. butter or margarine

Cook the onion in butter in a saucepan until tender but not brown. Cool. Prepare the hot roll mix according to package directions, adding onion to the dry mix. Cover and let rise in a warm place until doubled in bulk. Shape into 12 round buns. Place on a greased baking sheet and flatten slightly. Cover and let rise until almost doubled in bulk. Bake at 375 degrees for 20 to 25 minutes. 1 dozen.

Mrs. Becky Angelos, Oklahoma City, Oklahoma

QUICK ROLLS

2 c. packaged biscuit mix   2 tbsp. sugar
1 pkg. dry yeast   1/2 c. melted butter
1/2 c. water

Mix the biscuit mix and yeast in a bowl. Add the water and sugar and mix well. Let rise for 15 minutes. Knead on a floured surface, then roll out 1/2 inch thick. Cut with a biscuit cutter and place on a greased baking sheet. Let rise for 15 minutes. Brush with butter and fold in half. Bake at 450 degrees for 10 minutes or until golden brown. 10 rolls.

Mrs. Don Holt, Loudon, Tennessee

PECAN ROLLS

1 pkg. hot roll mix   2/3 c. pecans
6 tbsp. butter or margarine   1/2 c. sugar
1 c. (packed) brown sugar   1 1/2 tsp. cinnamon
1/2 c. dark corn syrup

Prepare the hot roll mix and let rise according to package directions. Melt 1/4 cup butter in a saucepan. Add the brown sugar and corn syrup and heat and stir until blended. Pour into two 9 1/2 x 5 x 3-inch loaf pans and sprinkle 1/3 cup pecans in each pan. Roll dough out on a lightly floured surface to a 24 x 12-inch rectangle and spread with remaining butter. Mix the sugar and cinnamon and sprinkle on the dough. Roll as for jelly roll, beginning at long side. Cut in 20 slices and place, cut side down, in prepared pans. Let rise for about 40 minutes. Bake at 375 degrees for about 25 minutes. Cool for 5 minutes and invert onto a rack. Remove pans.

Mrs. Russ Bradley, Greenville, South Carolina

LEMON CRESCENTS

1 pkg. hot roll mix	2 tbsp. lemon juice
1/2 c. margarine	1 egg, beaten

Prepare the roll mix and let rise according to package directions. Knead on a floured surface until smooth and elastic, then roll out to a 12-inch square. Cream the margarine. Add the lemon juice and mix well. Spread on the dough. Cut the dough in half. Cut each rectangle crosswise into 3-inch lengths, then cut each length into 2 triangles. Roll from 3-inch side to point. Place on a greased baking sheet, point side down, and shape into crescents. Let rise until doubled in bulk. Brush with egg. Bake in 450-degree oven for about 10 minutes or until brown.

pancakes
& waffles

WITH MIXES

Is there a family that doesn't love pancakes and waffles? Southern homemakers would overwhelmingly answer "no" to that question. Yet there inevitably comes a morning when the request for pancakes or waffles must be parried with a comment on your lack of time.

No more. Not with the seconds-to-prepare recipes you'll find in this section. Made with prepackaged mixes, these recipes have been especially designed to bring all the flavor excitement of pancakes and waffles made from scratch – without taking the time such foods require. In these pages, you'll discover family-approved recipes for Cheese-filled Roll-ups, the perfect accompaniment to a supper of leftovers . . . Delightful Orange Pancakes . . . Deviled Waffles . . . even a recipe for Peanut Butter Waffles certain to be a hit with the younger set!

Don't overlook the possibilities of creating smashing desserts in minutes, too. Pecan Waffles served with a topping of whipped cream or butterscotch sauce would certainly bring happy smiles your way. So would Pancakes with Peach Sauce – and the recipes for both are just waiting for you to discover them in the pages that follow.

Why not explore this section now, and serve your family a quick and easy pancake or waffle dish – today!

DOUBLE BLUEBERRY PANCAKES

1 c. milk	1 c. pancake mix
2 tbsp. light corn syrup	1/3 c. cottage cheese
1 tbsp. corn oil	Blueberry syrup
1 egg	

Combine the milk, corn syrup, corn oil and egg in a mixing bowl. Add the pancake mix and stir until dry ingredients are moistened. Batter will be lumpy. Add the cottage cheese and mix. Pour 1/4 cup batter for each pancake on a hot griddle and cook until brown, turning once. Serve with blueberry syrup. 8 pancakes.

Photograph for this recipe on page 146.

APPLE PANCAKES

2 c. packaged biscuit mix	2 c. grated apples
1 egg	2 tbsp. sugar
1 2/3 c. milk	1 tbsp. lemon juice

Place the biscuit mix, egg and milk in a bowl and beat with a rotary beater until smooth. Add the apples, sugar and lemon juice and mix well. Drop by spoonfuls onto a hot, greased pancake griddle and cook until bubbles cover the surface. Turn and brown on other side. Serve with syrup.

Jo Ellen Snead, Wilmington, Delaware

CHEESE-FILLED ROLL-UPS

2/3 c. milk	1 egg, well beaten
1 1/2 tbsp. butter	Cheese Filling
1/3 c. pancake mix	Orange Sauce

Place the milk and butter in a saucepan and heat until butter melts. Cool to lukewarm. Blend milk mixture and pancake mix into the egg in a bowl. Grease a small skillet lightly and heat. Pour in 2 tablespoons batter. Remove the skillet from heat and tip from side to side so batter covers skillet. Return to heat and cook until lightly browned. Remove from skillet. Fry remaining pancakes and stack until ready to fill. Spoon 2 tablespoons Cheese Filling across center of unbaked side of each pancake and roll up. Place, folded side down, in a skillet. Pour Orange Sauce over pancakes and heat until sauce bubbles. Serve warm. 8 servings.

Cheese Filling

2 3-oz. packages cream cheese	1 1/2 tbsp. orange juice
2 tbsp. sugar	2 tbsp. chopped pecans
2 1/4 tsp. grated orange rind	1/4 c. chopped dates (opt.)

Soften the cream cheese in a bowl, then blend in the sugar, orange rind, orange juice, pecans and dates. Beat until light.

Orange Sauce

1/2 c. sugar	1 1/2 c. orange juice
1 1/2 tbsp. cornstarch	1/4 c. chopped pecans
Dash of salt	2 tbsp. butter

Mix the sugar, cornstarch and salt in a bowl and stir in 1/4 cup orange juice. Bring remaining orange juice to a boil in a saucepan and stir in the sugar mixture. Cook, stirring, until thickened and clear. Remove from heat and stir in the pecans and butter until butter is melted.

Carrie Plant, Charleston, West Virginia

LEMON PANCAKES

1/2 pkg. pancake mix	Grated rind of 1 lemon
2 tbsp. margarine	2 tsp. sugar
1 1-pt. block lemon ice cream	

Prepare the pancake mix and cook according to package directions. Spread with margarine and keep warm. Cut the ice cream into thin slices and place 1 slice on each pancake. Roll pancakes and place on a platter. Sprinkle with lemon rind and sugar and serve immediately.

BLUEBERRY PANCAKES

2 c. prepared biscuit mix	1 c. drained blueberries
1 egg	2 tbsp. sugar
1 2/3 c. milk	

Place the biscuit mix, egg and milk in a bowl and beat until smooth. Add the blueberries and sugar and mix well. Pour 1/4 cup batter for each pancake onto a greased, hot griddle and cook until brown on both sides, turning once. Serve with butter and syrup, if desired.

Mrs. M. T. Barlow, Memphis, Tennessee

COCONUT PANCAKES

1 c. shredded coconut	1 egg
2 c. packaged biscuit mix	1 2/3 c. milk

Spread the coconut on a baking sheet. Bake at 350 degrees for 10 to 15 minutes or until lightly browned. Place the biscuit mix, egg and milk in a bowl and beat with a rotary beater until smooth. Stir in the coconut. Drop by spoonfuls onto a hot, greased griddle and cook until bubbles cover surface. Turn and brown on other side. Serve with maple syrup, if desired.

Mrs. F. B. Lowell, Hattiesburg, Mississippi

CORNMEAL PANCAKES

1 1/2 c. self-rising cornmeal	6 tbsp. salad oil or melted
1 1/2 c. pancake mix	shortening
3 eggs, slightly beaten	3 c. (about) milk

Mix the cornmeal and pancake mix in a bowl. Add the eggs, oil and milk and mix until almost smooth. Mixture will be lumpy. Drop by spoonfuls onto a greased hot griddle or skillet and cook until brown on both sides, turning once.

Mrs. H. F. Glenn, Huntsville, Alabama

ORANGE-PECAN PANCAKES

2 c. packaged biscuit mix	2 tsp. grated orange rind
1 egg	1/3 c. finely chopped pecans
1 2/3 c. milk	

Place the biscuit mix, egg and milk in a bowl and beat until smooth. Add the grated rind and pecans and mix well. Drop by spoonfuls onto a hot, greased griddle and cook until brown on both sides, turning once. Serve with maple syrup, if desired.

Lynn Allendale, Winston-Salem, North Carolina

PANCAKES WITH PEACH SAUCE

1 12-oz. package frozen
    peaches
2 c. milk
1 egg, slightly beaten
2 tbsp. melted shortening
2 c. pancake mix

1/2 c. finely chopped pecans
1/4 c. sugar
1 tbsp. cornstarch
1/4 c. water
2 tsp. lemon juice

Thaw the peaches. Drain and reserve syrup. Chop the peaches. Combine the milk, egg and shortening in a bowl and stir in the pancake mix. Pour 1/4 cup batter for each pancake onto a hot, lightly greased griddle and sprinkle each with about 1/2 tablespoon pecans. Cook until golden brown on each side, turning once. Keep warm. Mix the sugar and cornstarch in a saucepan. Stir in the water, peaches and reserved peach syrup and cook, stirring, until mixture comes to a boil. Boil for 1 minute. Remove from heat and stir in the lemon juice. Serve with pancakes.

Gayle Wilder, Arlington, Virginia

SOURDOUGH PANCAKES

4 c. biscuit mix
2 pkg. yeast
2 c. milk

1 1/3 c. water
2 eggs, at room temperature

Mix the biscuit mix and undissolved yeast thoroughly in a large bowl. Combine the milk and water in a saucepan and place over low heat until liquids are warm. Add to dry ingredients gradually and beat for 1 minute with electric mixer at low speed, scraping bowl occasionally. Add the eggs and continue beating at the same speed for 1 minute, scraping bowl occasionally. Cover and let stand at room temperature for 30 minutes. Stir down. Bake on lightly greased hot griddle, using about 1/4 cup batter for each pancake. Stir down batter occasionally as used. About 26 pancakes.

GINGER-PRUNE PANCAKES

2 c. packaged biscuit mix	1/2 c. chopped prunes
1 egg	1/2 c. chopped nuts
1 2/3 c. milk	1/2 tsp. ginger

Mix the biscuit mix, egg and milk in a bowl until smooth. Add the prunes, nuts and ginger and mix well. Drop by spoonfuls onto a hot, greased griddle and cook until brown on both sides, turning once. Serve with syrup.

Mrs. L. A. Bailey, Cumberland, Maryland

ORANGE RICOTTA PANCAKES

1 c. pancake mix	2 tsp. grated Florida orange rind
Florida orange juice	
1/2 c. sugar	1/4 c. Marsala wine
1 tbsp. cornstarch	2 Florida oranges, sectioned
1/4 tsp. salt	2 c. ricotta cheese
2 tbsp. butter or margarine	

Prepare the pancake mix according to package directions, substituting orange juice for half the liquid. Cook, one at a time, on a hot griddle, using a scant 1/2 cup batter for each pancake. Keep warm. Mix the sugar, cornstarch and salt in a saucepan. Stir in 3/4 cup orange juice gradually and cook over medium heat, stirring constantly, until mixture thickens and comes to a boil. Stir in the butter, orange rind and wine. Add orange sections and heat through. Stack pancakes, spreading about 1/3 cup ricotta cheese between each layer and drizzling with a small amount of orange sauce. Pile remaining ricotta cheese on top and add some of the orange sauce. Cut in wedges and serve with remaining sauce. Creamed cottage cheese may be substituted for ricotta cheese. 4 servings.

DELIGHTFUL ORANGE PANCAKES

1 egg, beaten
1 c. light cream
1 6-oz. can frozen orange
   juice concentrate, thawed

1 c. pancake mix
1/2 c. butter or margarine
1 c. sugar

Combine the egg, cream and 1/4 cup orange juice concentrate in a bowl. Add the pancake mix and stir until most of the lumps are gone. Drop by spoonfuls onto a hot, greased griddle and cook until brown on both sides, turning once. Combine the butter, sugar and remaining orange juice concentrate and heat to boiling point, stirring occasionally. Serve with pancakes.

Mrs. Julie Vernon, New Orleans, Louisiana

CREAM CHEESE PANCAKES WITH SYRUP

2 eggs
2 c. milk
2 c. packaged biscuit mix

2 3-oz. packages cream cheese
1/4 c. cream
Syrup

Place the eggs, milk and biscuit mix in a bowl and beat with a rotary beater until smooth. Spoon 3 tablespoons at a time, into a lightly greased 6-inch skillet and tilt the skillet to coat bottom. Cook until bubbles cover the surface, then turn and brown on other side. Soften the cream cheese in a bowl. Add the cream slowly and mix until smooth. Spread on the pancakes. Roll up pancakes and place in a single layer in a baking pan, folded side down. Bake at 400 degrees for 10 minutes to reheat and serve with warm Syrup.

Syrup

2 c. sugar
1 6-oz. can frozen pineapple
   juice concentrate

1/2 c. butter
1/4 c. water

Mix all ingredients in a saucepan and bring to a boil. Cook for 5 minutes. Remove from heat and cool slightly.

Mrs. Floyd Lyles, Greenwood, South Carolina

ORANGE PANCAKES

1/2 c. orange juice
1/2 c. milk
1 egg

2 tbsp. salad oil
1 tsp. grated orange peel
1 c. packaged pancake mix

Combine the orange juice, milk, egg, salad oil and orange peel in a bowl. Add the pancake mix and stir until most of the lumps are gone. Drop by spoonfuls onto a greased, hot griddle and cook until bubbles cover surface. Turn and brown on other side. Serve with syrup. 12-14 small pancakes.

Mrs. Gene Conway, Cordell, Oklahoma

ROLLED APRICOT PANCAKES

1 c. packaged pancake mix	1/2 c. apricot jam
1 c. milk	2 eggs, slightly beaten
1 egg	1/2 c. corn flake crumbs
1 tbsp. salad oil	2 tbsp. butter or margarine

Mix the pancake mix, milk, egg and oil in a bowl until smooth. Bake on griddle according to package directions. Spread 1 tablespoon jam over each pancake and roll up. Dip in eggs, then in corn flake crumbs and place, seam side down, in a heated skillet containing the butter. Brown on all sides over low heat. Serve hot with melted butter, if desired. 8 pancakes.

Louise Miles, Newark, Delaware

SOURDOUGH PANCAKES

1 pkg. dry yeast	2 c. milk
1/4 c. warm water	2 c. packaged biscuit mix
1 egg	

Dissolve the yeast in the water. Beat the egg in a bowl. Add the milk and biscuit mix and beat with a rotary beater until blended. Stir in the yeast. Let stand at room temperature for 1 hour to 1 hour and 30 minutes without stirring. Pour 1/4 cup batter for each pancake onto a hot, lightly greased griddle and cook until top side is bubbly. Turn and brown on other side. About 2 dozen 4-inch pancakes.

Mrs. H. W. Boone, Barbourville, Kentucky

BACON WAFFLES

2 c. packaged biscuit mix	2 tbsp. salad oil
1 egg	1/3 c. crisp crumbled bacon
1 2/3 c. milk	

Combine the biscuit mix, egg, milk and oil in a bowl and beat with a rotary beater until smooth. Stir in the bacon. Pour 1/3 of the batter into a hot 9-inch waffle iron and bake until brown. Repeat for remaining batter. Serve with maple syrup.

Carol Nelson, Charleston, West Virginia

BACON-PEANUT BUTTER WAFFLES

4 c. pancake mix	1 c. crisp bacon, crumbled
1 c. peanut butter	

Prepare the pancake mix according to package directions for waffles. Blend in the peanut butter and fold in bacon. Bake according to package directions for waffles. 4-6 waffles.

Fay Huffines, Turkey, Texas

BLUEBERRY WAFFLES

2 c. packaged biscuit mix
1 egg
1 2/3 c. milk

2 tbsp. salad oil
1 c. drained blueberries
2 tbsp. sugar

Place the biscuit mix, egg, milk and oil in a bowl and beat until smooth. Stir in the blueberries and sugar. Bake 3/4 cup batter at a time in a hot waffle iron until brown.

Mrs. J. B. Hampton, Hot Springs, Arkansas

WAFFLE HEARTS

2 c. sweetened whipped cream
1 c. fresh raspberries
3/4 c. strong brewed coffee
3/4 c. milk

1 c. sour cream
1 egg
1/4 c. salad oil
1 1/2 c. pancake mix

Mix the whipped cream and raspberries and chill. Combine the coffee, milk, sour cream, egg and oil in a bowl and blend well. Add the pancake mix and beat with an electric mixer until smooth. Pour enough batter into a hot waffle iron to spread to 1 inch from edge. Bake until steaming stops. Repeat with remaining batter. Cut the waffles in heart-shaped size. Serve with whipped cream mixture. One-half cup raspberry jam may be substituted for fresh raspberries.

BANANA WAFFLES

2 c. packaged biscuit mix
1 egg
1 2/3 c. milk
2 tbsp. salad oil

2 med. bananas, mashed
1 tbsp. lemon juice
2 tbsp. sugar

Place the biscuit mix, egg, milk and oil in a bowl and beat with an electric mixer or rotary beater until smooth. Add the bananas, lemon juice and sugar and mix well. Bake 3/4 cup batter at a time in a hot waffle iron until brown. Serve with jelly or syrup.

Mrs. Robert Quimby, Meridian, Mississippi

CRISP WAFFLES

2 tbsp. melted shortening
1 1/2 c. pancake mix

1 egg
1 1/4 c. milk

Mix the shortening, pancake mix, egg and milk in a bowl until smooth. Bake 1/2 cup batter at a time in a hot waffle iron for 10 minutes.

Clara Thompson, Abbeville, Mississippi

DESSERT CREAM WAFFLES

3 eggs, separated
1 1/2 c. heavy cream
1 tsp. vanilla

2 c. packaged biscuit mix
1 tbsp. sugar

Beat the egg yolks in a bowl. Add the cream and vanilla and mix well. Stir in the biscuit mix and sugar until smooth. Beat the egg whites until soft peaks form and fold into the cream mixture. Bake in heated waffle iron and serve immediately. Three 9-inch waffles.

Mrs. Charlotte Painter, Baton Rouge, Louisiana

DEVILED WAFFLES

2 eggs
1 1/2 c. milk
2 tsp. melted shortening
1 c. pancake mix

1 c. instant hot whole wheat
 cereal
2 4 1/2-oz. cans deviled ham

Beat the eggs, milk and shortening in a bowl until mixed. Add the pancake mix and cereal and mix well. Stir in the deviled ham. Pour 1/2 cup batter for each waffle into a hot waffle iron and bake until brown.

Mrs. W. R. Lowrey, Warner Robins, Georgia

FLUFFY WAFFLES

2 eggs, separated	2 tbsp. sugar
1 c. milk	1/4 c. salad oil
2 1/3 c. prepared biscuit mix	

Beat the egg yolks in a bowl with a rotary beater until light, then blend in the milk. Add the biscuit mix and sugar and mix just until biscuit mix is moistened. Stir in the oil. Fold in the stiffly beaten egg whites. Spoon 3/4 cup batter at a time into heated waffle iron. Bake until steaming stops and waffles are golden brown and serve hot.

Mildred Jenkins, Montgomery, Alabama

PECAN WAFFLES

2 c. packaged biscuit mix	2 tbsp. salad oil
1 egg	3/4 c. finely chopped pecans
1 2/3 c. milk	

Place all ingredients in a bowl and beat with a rotary beater until well mixed. Pour 3/4 cup batter at a time into a hot waffle iron and bake until brown. Serve with syrup.

Mrs. Edith Rucker, Cocoa, Florida

PEANUT BUTTER WAFFLES

1 c. packaged pancake mix	1 egg
2 tbsp. sugar	1 c. milk
1/3 c. chunk-style peanut butter	2 tbsp. salad oil

Combine all ingredients in a bowl and beat with a rotary beater or electric mixer until almost smooth. Mixture will be lumpy. Bake in a hot waffle iron until brown. Serve with butter and jelly, if desired. Eight 4-inch waffles.

Mrs. C. F. Meredith, Flagstaff, Arizona

SPICY WAFFLES

2 c. packaged biscuit mix	1 tsp. cinnamon
1 egg	1/2 tsp. allspice
1 2/3 c. milk	1/2 tsp. cloves
2 tbsp. salad oil	1/2 tsp. nutmeg

Place all ingredients in a bowl and beat with a rotary beater until smooth. Bake in a hot waffle iron until brown. Serve with syrup. Three 9-inch waffles.

Mrs. L. F. Hayes, Albuquerque, New Mexico

foreign
breads

Down through the years, hospitable Southerners have welcomed many newcomers into their region and shared with them homes, furnishings, even food. In turn, many newcomers enriched southern cookery with recipes brought from their native lands. Almost every nation has its traditional bread recipes, and the finest of these, especially adapted by southern women for American tastes, are included in the pages that follow.

From central Europe have come recipes older than the Austro-Hungarian empire — the regime which established this part of Europe as the world's baking capital. Austrian Kugelhupf and Czechoslovakian Kolaches are just two time-honored recipes you'll discover in the exciting pages that follow. And the British Isles supplied such recipes as English Yorkshire Pudding, a great complement to any beef dish . . . Irish Soda Bread, stuffed with raisins and caraway seeds . . . and Scotch Shortbread. The French and Germans too, were important in settling the South, and from their cuisines have come recipes for French Savarin Cake and German Stollen.

The next time appetites flag at your house, introduce your family to the international world of breads with the recipes in this section . . . home-tested recipes certain to be a hit with everyone!

AUSTRIAN HONEY-NUT BREAD

2 1/2 c. sifted flour	1 lge. egg
1 tsp. salt	3/4 c. buttermilk or sour milk
1 tsp. soda	3/4 c. white raisins (opt.)
2 1/2 tbsp. butter	3/4 c. chopped nuts
1 c. honey	

Sift the flour, salt and soda together. Cream the butter and honey in a bowl. Add the egg and mix. Add sifted ingredients alternately with the buttermilk. Stir in the raisins and nuts and pour into a greased loaf pan. Bake at 300 degrees for 1 hour and 40 minutes.

Mrs. Frank Baldwin, Lubbock, Texas

FINNISH RIESKA BREAD

1 c. lukewarm milk	2 tsp. salt
1 c. lukewarm water	2 c. barley flour
1 pkg. yeast	2 1/2 c. flour

Pour the milk and water into a bowl. Add the yeast and salt and mix until yeast is dissolved. Add the barley flour and mix well. Cover with a towel and let rise for 1 hour or until doubled in bulk. Add the flour and mix until smooth. Let rise for 30 minutes. Knead on a pastry board until smooth. Divide in 2 parts and shape each part into a round 8-inch loaf. Place on a baking sheet and let rise for about 1 hour or until doubled in bulk. Prick the loaves with a fork. Bake in 400-degree oven for 15 to 20 minutes or until done. Cool.

AUSTRIAN KUGELHUPF

1/2 c. milk, scalded	2 eggs, beaten
1/2 c. sugar	2 c. unsifted flour
1/2 tsp. salt	2 tbsp. fine bread crumbs
1/4 c. margarine	14 whole blanched almonds
1 pkg. yeast	1/2 c. seedless raisins
1/4 c. warm water	1/2 tsp. grated lemon rind

Mix the milk, sugar, salt and margarine in a bowl and cool to lukewarm. Dissolve the yeast in the water, then stir into the milk mixture. Add the eggs and flour and beat vigorously for about 5 minutes. Cover and let rise in a warm place, free from draft, for about 1 hour and 30 minutes or until doubled in bulk. Sprinkle the bread crumbs over sides and bottom of well-greased 1 1/2-quart casserole and arrange the almonds on bottom. Stir the dough down and beat well. Stir in the raisins and grated rind and place in the casserole. Let rise in a warm place for about 1 hour or until doubled in bulk. Bake at 350 degrees for about 50 minutes.

Lula Smith, Sand Springs, Oklahoma

BRAZILIAN BOLO DE CAFE

1 c. seedless raisins	1 1/2 c. sifted flour
2/3 c. strong coffee	1/2 tsp. baking powder
1/2 tsp. cinnamon	1/2 tsp. soda
2/3 c. shortening	1/4 tsp. salt
1 c. sugar	1/2 c. chopped nuts
2 eggs	1 1/2 c. powdered sugar

Combine the raisins, coffee and cinnamon and set aside. Cream the shortening and sugar in a bowl. Add the eggs, one at a time, beating well after each addition. Sift dry ingredients together and stir into egg mixture alternately with coffee mixture. Stir in the nuts. Spread in a greased 10 x 15 x 1-inch jelly roll pan. Bake at 350 degrees for 20 to 25 minutes. Add enough additional coffee to powdered sugar to make a thin frosting and spread on the warm baked mixture. Cool, then cut into 36 bars.

Mary Janice Johnson, Richardson, Texas

CANADIAN POPOVERS

3 eggs	1 c. sifted flour
1 c. milk	1/8 tsp. salt

Beat the eggs in a bowl until thick and lemon colored. Add the milk and beat well. Sift the flour with the salt. Add to egg mixture and beat until smooth. Fill large, well-greased muffin cups 2/3 full. Bake at 425 degrees for 15 minutes. Reduce temperature to 350 degrees and bake for 30 minutes longer.

Mrs. Sandy North, Hickory, North Carolina

CZECHOSLOVAKIAN COTTAGE KOLACHES

2 1/2 c. sifted all-purpose flour	2 c. creamed cottage cheese
2 tsp. baking powder	1 c. butter
3 tbsp. sugar	2 eggs, beaten
1/2 tsp. salt	Fruit fillings
	Confectioners' sugar

Sift the flour, baking powder, sugar and salt together. Beat the cottage cheese in a bowl until smooth and creamy. Add the butter and beat until light and fluffy. Stir in the sifted ingredients. Add the eggs and mix well. Wrap in plastic wrap or waxed paper and chill thoroughly. Roll out 1/8 inch thick on a floured surface and cut into 3-inch squares. Place 1 spoon filling in center of each square. Fold over corners and pinch together. Place on baking sheets. Bake in 375-degree oven for 18 to 20 minutes or until golden brown. Dust with confectioners' sugar and cool on wire racks. About 2 1/2 dozen.

SLAVIC APRICOT KOLACHES

1 1/2 pkg. dry yeast	2 tsp. salt
2 c. lukewarm milk	5 1/2 to 6 c. all-purpose flour
1/2 c. shortening	Melted margarine
1/2 c. sugar	Apricot or prune filling
3 egg yolks, beaten	

Dissolve the yeast in the milk in a bowl. Add the shortening, sugar, egg yolks and salt and mix well. Add the flour gradually and stir until smooth. Brush with margarine and let rise until doubled in bulk. Shape into balls and roll in the margarine. Place on a baking sheet and let rise until doubled in bulk. Make an indentation in the center and fill with apricot filling. Let rise for about 20 minutes. Bake in 375-degree oven until brown. Brush with margarine and cool.

Mrs. Fred A. Havel, Jr., Gonzales, Texas

DANISH PUFFS

Margarine	3 eggs
2 c. sifted flour	2 c. confectioners' sugar
2 tbsp. cold water	1/4 c. cream or milk
1 c. boiling water	1 tsp. vanilla
1 tsp. almond flavoring	1/8 tsp. salt

Cut 1/2 cup margarine into 1 cup flour in a bowl until mixture resembles coarse cornmeal. Add the cold water and stir until well blended. Divide in half and press each half into a greased cookie pan. Add 1/2 cup margarine to the boiling water in a saucepan and bring to a boil. Add the almond flavoring and remove from heat. Stir in remaining flour. Add the eggs, one at a time, beating well after each addition. Spread over mixture in the cookie pans. Bake in 400-degree oven for about 45 minutes, then cut into bars. Mix 1 tablespoon margarine and remaining ingredients in a bowl and frost bars while hot. Serve warm.

Mrs. Warren Longworth, Cape Charles, Virginia

ENGLISH CRUMPETS

2 pkg. yeast	1 tbsp. salt
4 c. lukewarm water	Butter
4 c. sifted flour	

Dissolve the yeast in the water in a bowl. Add flour and salt and beat well. Cover and let rise in a warm place for about 1 hour or until doubled in bulk. Beat well. Fill greased muffin tins 1/2 full. Place on a griddle over medium heat and cook until bubbles rise to top and break. Cut through crumpets from top to bottom. Reduce heat to low and cook until tops are dry and sides shrink slightly. Toast on unbrowned side and spread with butter before serving.

Mrs. G. L. Samford, Pasadena, Maryland

ENGLISH YORKSHIRE PUDDING

1 c. all-purpose flour	2 eggs, well beaten
1 tsp. salt	1/4 c. roast drippings or
1 tbsp. shortening	salad oil
1 c. milk	

Sift the flour and salt together into a bowl and cut in the shortening. Add the milk and eggs and beat with electric mixer at high speed for 10 minutes. Chill thoroughly. Heat a muffin pan until very hot and pour 1 teaspoon roast drippings into each cup. Fill each cup 1/2 full with batter. Bake at 425 degrees for 30 minutes. 12 muffins.

Mrs. J. K. Willman, Wilmington, Delaware

FINNISH CARDAMOM BREAD

3 pkg. dry yeast	5/8 c. sugar
1/2 c. warm water	2 tsp. finely ground cardamom
1/2 c. milk, scalded	3 lge. eggs, beaten
5 tbsp. butter	4 1/2 to 5 c. sifted flour
1 1/2 tsp. salt	1 egg white

Dissolve the yeast in the warm water. Mix the milk, butter, salt and 1/2 cup sugar in a bowl and cool until lukewarm. Add the yeast, cardamom and eggs and mix lightly. Add enough flour to make a stiff dough and knead on a floured surface for 5 to 8 minutes. Place in a greased bowl and cover. Let rise in a warm place for 45 minutes. Punch down and divide into 3 parts. Roll each part into a long roll and place rolls close together on a greased cookie sheet. Braid the rolls. Beat the egg white with remaining sugar until stiff and spread on the braid. Cover and let rise for 45 to 50 minutes. Bake in 375-degree oven for about 40 minutes or until toothpick inserted in center comes out clean.

Mrs. Anne Arnett Sutherland, Lithonia, Georgia

FRENCH SAVARIN CAKE

2 pkg. yeast	4 c. (about) sifted flour
1/4 c. lukewarm water	1 1/2 tsp. vanilla
1/2 c. milk, scalded	4 eggs, beaten
1/3 c. sugar	Confectioners' sugar icing
1 tsp. salt	Almonds
2/3 c. melted butter	Candied fruits

Dissolve the yeast in water. Mix the milk, sugar, salt and butter in a bowl and cool to lukewarm. Add enough flour to make a medium dough and mix well. Add the yeast, vanilla and eggs and beat well. Add enough flour to make a stiff dough and beat until smooth. Cover and let rise in a warm place until doubled in bulk. Punch down. Turn into a well-greased 10-inch tube pan and let rise until doubled in bulk. Bake at 350 degrees for 35 minutes. Remove from pan and cool. Drizzle with confectioners' sugar icing and decorate with almonds and fruits. 12-15 servings.

Mrs. D. T. Hamilton, Michie, Tennessee

FRENCH LOAVES

1 pkg. yeast	1 tsp. salt
3/4 c. melted butter or	6 c. flour
margarine	1 egg, beaten
2 c. lukewarm milk	

Place the yeast in a bowl. Mix the butter and milk. Pour over the yeast and stir until dissolved. Add the salt and flour and mix until smooth. Let rise until doubled in bulk. Knead on a floured board until smooth. Reserve 1 cup dough. Divide remaining dough in half and shape each half into an oblong loaf. Place on a baking sheet. Divide reserved dough in half and shape each half into a roll the length of loaves. Twist, then place each roll on a loaf. Let rise until doubled in bulk. Brush with egg. Bake in 350-degree oven for about 20 minutes.

Photograph for this recipe on page 1.

BLUEBERRY BRIOCHE

2 c. fresh blueberries	1/4 c. butter
1 pkg. dry yeast	1 tsp. salt
1/4 c. lukewarm water	2 eggs, well beaten
3/4 c. scalded milk	4 c. (about) sifted flour
1/2 c. sugar	1/2 tsp. ground cinnamon

Rinse and drain the blueberries. Sprinkle yeast into lukewarm water in a bowl and let stand without stirring for 5 minutes. Stir to mix well. Mix the milk with 1/4 cup sugar, butter, salt and 1 egg in a large bowl and cool to lukewarm. Stir in the yeast. Add enough flour to make a stiff dough and mix well. Knead on a lightly floured board until smooth and elastic, then place in the bowl. Cover and let rise until doubled in bulk. Punch down. Cut off a piece of dough the size of a small apple and reserve for top. Pat out remaining dough on the floured board into a rectangle and sprinkle with blueberries, remaining sugar and cinnamon. Roll as for jelly roll and shape into a large ball by pulling in the sides. Place the dough, seam side down, in a greased 8-inch fluted pan. Make an indentation in center of the top. Shape reserved dough into a ball and place in the indentation. Brush entire surface with remaining egg and let rise until doubled in bulk. Bake in a 350-degree oven for 45 to 55 minutes or until top is deep brown and the brioche sounds hollow when thumped. Cool in the pan slightly, then unmold by loosening the edges. Cut into wedges and serve warm with whipped butter, if desired.

GERMAN BLUEBERRY KUCHEN

3 c. sifted all-purpose flour	2 eggs
1 3/4 c. sugar	2 tsp. vanilla
4 tsp. baking powder	1 tsp. ground nutmeg
1/2 tsp. salt	Grated rind of 1 lemon
1/2 c. vegetable shortening	2 c. blueberries
1 1/3 c. milk	Confectioners' sugar

Preheat oven to 350 degrees. Combine the flour, 1 1/2 cups sugar, baking powder and salt in a bowl. Add the shortening and milk and beat for 3 minutes with an electric mixer or beat 300 strokes by hand. Add the eggs, vanilla, nutmeg and lemon rind and beat for 2 minutes or 200 strokes. Pour into a greased and floured 13 x 9 x 2-inch pan and sprinkle with blueberries and remaining sugar. Bake for 40 to 45 minutes or until lightly browned. Cool slightly in pan, then cut into squares. Sprinkle with confectioners' sugar and serve warm.

GERMAN STOLLEN

1 pkg. dry yeast	4 to 4 1/2 c. sifted flour
1/4 c. warm water	1 egg, slightly beaten
1 c. scalded milk	1 c. seedless raisins
1/2 c. butter or margarine	1/4 c. currants
1/4 c. sugar	1/4 c. chopped mixed
1 tsp. salt	candied fruits
1/4 tsp. ground cardamom	2 tbsp. grated orange peel

1 tbsp. grated lemon peel	Glaze
1/4 c. chopped blanched	Citron
almonds	Candied cherries

Dissolve the yeast in the water. Combine the milk, butter, sugar, salt and cardamom in a bowl and cool to lukewarm. Stir in 2 cups flour and beat well. Add the yeast and egg and beat well. Stir in the fruits, peels and almonds, then stir in enough remaining flour to make soft dough. Turn out on lightly floured surface and knead for 8 to 10 minutes or until smooth and elastic. Place in a greased bowl, turning once to grease surface, and cover. Let rise in a warm place for 1 hour and 45 minutes or until doubled in bulk. Punch down and turn out on a lightly floured surface. Divide in 3 equal portions and cover. Let rest for 10 minutes. Roll out each portion to a 10 x 6-inch rectangle. Fold the long side over to within 1 inch of the opposite side. Fold remaining long side over and seal. Place on a greased baking sheets and cover. Let rise in a warm place for 1 hour or until doubled in bulk. Bake at 375 degrees for 15 to 20 minutes or until golden brown. Brush with Glaze while warm. Cut holly leaves and berries from citron and bits of cut-up candied cherries and place on Stollen.

Glaze

1 c. sifted confectioners'	2 tbsp. hot water
sugar	1 tsp. butter

Combine the sugar, hot water and butter in a bowl and mix well.

Mrs. Camilla Vincent, Meridian, Mississippi

GERMAN SCHNECKEN

2 pkg. dry yeast	6 1/2 c. sifted flour
1 c. warm water	2 c. (firmly packed) brown
1 c. sugar	sugar
1 c. shortening	1 1/2 tsp. cinnamon
1 tsp. salt	Melted butter or margarine
1 c. boiling water	1 c. seedless raisins
2 eggs, slightly beaten	1 c. chopped nuts

Dissolve the yeast in warm water. Combine the sugar, shortening and salt in a large mixing bowl. Add the boiling water and stir until shortening is melted. Cool to lukewarm. Add the eggs and yeast and mix well. Add 4 cups flour and beat until smooth. Add remaining flour gradually and beat until smooth. Chill for at least 4 hours. Divide dough in half and roll out each half on a floured surface to an 18 x 10-inch rectangle. Combine the brown sugar, cinnamon and 3/4 cup melted butter and sprinkle 1/4 of the mixture over each rectangle. Top each with half the raisins and nuts. Roll as for jelly roll, starting with long side, then cut into 1 1/2-inch slices. Sprinkle remaining brown sugar mixture into 2 dozen 3-inch muffin cups. Place slices, cut-side down, in cups. Cover and let rise in a warm place for about 1 hour and 15 minutes or until doubled in bulk. Brush with melted butter. Bake at 375 degrees for 20 to 25 minutes. Remove from oven and invert onto a large tray.

Mrs. David Knott, Laredo, Texas

GREEK PSOMI ELLENIKA GIORTI

1/4 c. milk, scalded	2 cinnamon sticks
1 pkg. yeast	1 c. boiling water
1/4 lb. butter	1/4 tsp. baking powder
3/4 c. sugar	5 to 6 c. flour
3 eggs, beaten	1 egg yolk, beaten
1/2 c. mashed potato	

Cool the milk to lukewarm. Add the yeast and stir until dissolved. Mix the butter and sugar well in a bowl. Add the eggs and blend thoroughly. Stir in the yeast mixture. Add potato and mix thoroughly. Add the cinnamon sticks to the boiling water in a saucepan and boil for 5 minutes. Cool until lukewarm. Remove the cinnamon sticks and stir liquid into the yeast mixture. Add the baking powder and enough flour to make a stiff dough and mix well. Knead on a floured surface until smooth. Place in a greased large bowl and cover. Let rise until doubled in bulk. Divide into 3 parts and shape each part into a long roll. Place close together on a greased baking sheet and braid. Brush top with egg yolk and garnish with walnuts or sesame seed. Bake at 350 degrees for 1 hour.

Mrs. N. S. Harrison, Wheeling, West Virginia

HUNGARIAN BUTTERHORNS

1 1/2 c. sugar	3 eggs, separated
4 c. sifted flour	1 c. sour cream
1/2 tsp. salt	Powdered sugar
1 c. butter	3/4 c. finely chopped nuts
1 pkg. yeast	Confectioners' icing
2 tsp. vanilla	

Sift 1/2 cup sugar, flour and salt together into a bowl and cut in the butter. Add the yeast, 1 teaspoon vanilla, beaten egg yolks and sour cream and mix until smooth. Divide into 10 parts. Roll out each part into a circle on a board covered with powdered sugar and cut into 8 pie-shaped wedges. Beat the egg whites until stiff, adding remaining sugar gradually, and fold in remaining vanilla. Place 1 teaspoon meringue on wide end of each wedge and roll towards point. Place on a greased baking sheet, point side down, and let rise for 30 minutes. Bake in a 400-degree oven until brown. Frost with confectioners' icing while warm.

Mrs. John O. Batiste, Fort Knox, Kentucky

HUNGARIAN COFFEE CAKE

1 pkg. dry yeast	1/4 c. soft shortening
1/4 c. warm water	3 1/2 to 3 3/4 c. sifted flour
3/4 c. lukewarm milk	1/2 c. melted butter
1 c. sugar	1 tsp. cinnamon
1 tsp. salt	1/2 c. finely chopped nuts
1 egg, beaten	1/2 c. seedless raisins

Dissolve the yeast in water in a mixing bowl and stir in the milk, 1/4 cup sugar and salt. Add egg, shortening and half the flour and mix well. Add enough remaining flour to make a stiff dough and mix well. Turn onto a lightly floured board and knead for about 5 minutes or until smooth. Place in a greased bowl and turn to grease surface. Cover with a damp cloth and let rise in a warm place for 1 hour and 30 minutes to 2 hours or until doubled in bulk. Punch down, then let rise for 30 to 40 minutes or until almost doubled in bulk. Shape into balls, using 2 tablespoons dough for each. Roll each ball in melted butter, then in a mixture of remaining sugar, cinnamon and nuts. Place half the balls in a well-greased tube pan and sprinkle with half the raisins. Repeat layers, pressing raisins in lightly. Let rise for 45 minutes. Bake at 375 degrees for 35 to 40 minutes. 6-8 servings.

Helen Janis Hale, Somerset, Kentucky

ICELANDIC PANCAKES

3 eggs	1/2 tsp. vanilla
2 c. milk	1 tbsp. sugar
1 c. flour	Melted butter or margarine
1/2 tsp. salt	

Combine all ingredients except butter in an electric blender and blend for several seconds. Heat a 6 or 8-inch skillet and brush lightly with butter. Pour the batter, 2 tablespoons at a time, into the skillet and tilt to cover bottom. Fry until lightly browned. Turn and brown on other side. Keep warm. Serve with syrup or whipped cream and fresh fruit. 6-7 servings.

Mrs. C. N. Sheridan, Tupelo, Mississippi

IRISH FRECKLE BREAD

4 3/4 to 5 3/4 c. unsifted flour	1/2 c. margarine
1/2 c. sugar	2 eggs, at room temperature
1 tsp. salt	1/4 c. warm mashed potatoes
2 pkg. dry yeast	1 c. seedless raisins
1 c. potato water or water	

Mix 1 1/2 cups flour, sugar, salt and undissolved yeast thoroughly in a large bowl. Combine the potato water and margarine in a saucepan and place over low heat until liquid is warm. Margarine does not need to melt. Add to dry ingredients gradually and beat for 2 minutes with electric mixer at medium speed, scraping bowl occasionally. Add the eggs, potatoes and 1/2 cup flour and beat at high speed for 2 minutes, scraping bowl occasionally. Stir in the raisins and enough remaining flour to make a soft dough. Turn out onto a lightly floured board and knead for 8 to 10 minutes or until smooth and elastic. Place in a greased bowl and turn to grease top. Cover and let rise in a warm place free from draft, for about 1 hour and 15 minutes or until doubled in bulk. Punch down. Turn out onto a lightly floured board and divide into 4 equal pieces. Shape each piece into a loaf about 8 1/2 inches long. Place 2 loaves, side by side, in each of 2 greased 8 1/2 x 4 1/2 x 2 1/2-inch loaf pans. Cover and let rise in a warm place, free from draft, for about 1 hour or until doubled in bulk. Bake in 350-degree oven for about 35 minutes or until done. Remove from pans and cool on wire racks.

Photograph for this recipe on page 158.

IRISH SODA BREAD

2 c. sifted flour
1 1/2 tsp. baking powder
3/4 tsp. soda
1 tsp. salt
3 tbsp. sugar

1 1/2 tsp. caraway seed
3 tbsp. shortening
1 c. buttermilk
2/3 c. chopped dark raisins
Melted butter

Sift the flour with baking powder, soda, salt and sugar into a bowl and add caraway seed. Cut in the shortening until mixture resembles meal. Make a well in center and pour in the buttermilk. Add the raisins and mix lightly. Turn out on a floured board and knead gently. Shape into a ball and fit into a greased 8 or 9-inch round cake pan. Cut loaf crosswise into quarters about 2/3 way through dough with a sharp knife or scissors. Brush top of loaf with melted butter and sprinkle with additional sugar. Bake in 350-degree oven for about 30 minutes.

MEXICAN JALAPENO CORN BREAD

1 c. cornmeal
3 tsp. baking powder
1 1/2 tsp. salt
2 eggs, beaten
1 c. sour cream

1/2 c. salad oil
1 c. cream-style corn
3 jalapeno peppers, minced
1 c. grated Cheddar cheese

Mix the cornmeal, baking powder and salt in a bowl. Add the eggs, sour cream, oil and corn and mix well. Pour half the batter into a greased, heated skillet and sprinkle with the jalapeno peppers and cheese. Cover with remaining batter. Bake at 350 degrees for 1 hour.

Mrs. John Melton, Bunker Hill, West Virginia

NORWEGIAN COUNTRY LOAVES

2 pkg. yeast	1/4 c. melted margarine
2 3/4 c. lukewarm milk	4 1/2 c. sifted rye flour
Molasses or corn syrup	3/4 c. whole wheat flour
1 tsp. salt	4 1/2 c. (about) flour

Dissolve the yeast in the milk in a large bowl and stir in 1 1/4 cups molasses, salt and margarine. Add the rye flour and whole wheat flour gradually and mix well. Add enough flour for a stiff dough and mix until smooth. Shape into 2 oblong loaves and place on greased baking sheets. Let rise until doubled in bulk. Dilute 2 tablespoons molasses with 1 tablespoon water and brush on loaves. Sprinkle with additional whole wheat flour. Bake at 350 degrees for about 45 minutes or until well browned. Wrap each loaf in a towel and cool.

Photograph for this recipe on page 1.

RUSSIAN BLACK BREAD

4 c. unsifted rye flour	1/2 tsp. crushed fennel seed
3 c. unsifted flour	2 pkg. dry yeast
1 tsp. sugar	1/4 c. vinegar
2 tsp. salt	1/4 c. dark molasses
2 c. whole bran cereal	1 1-oz. square unsweetened
2 tbsp. crushed caraway seed	chocolate
2 tsp. instant coffee	1/4 c. margarine
2 tsp. onion powder	1 tsp. cornstarch

Combine the rye flour and flour. Mix 2 1/3 cups flour mixture, sugar, salt, cereal, caraway seed, coffee, onion powder, fennel seed and undissolved yeast thoroughly in a large bowl. Combine 2 1/2 cups water, vinegar, molasses, chocolate and margarine in a saucepan and place over low heat until liquids are warm. Margarine and chocolate do not need to melt. Add to dry ingredients gradually and beat for 2 minutes with electric mixer at medium speed, scraping bowl occasionally. Add 1/2 cup flour mixture and beat at high speed for 2 minutes, scraping bowl occasionally. Stir in enough remaining flour mixture to make a soft dough. Turn out onto a lightly floured board. Cover dough with bowl and let rest for 15 minutes. Knead for 10 to 15 minutes or until smooth and elastic. Dough may be sticky. Place in a greased bowl and turn to grease top. Cover and let rise in warm place, free from draft, for about 1 hour or until doubled in bulk. Punch down. Turn out onto a lightly floured board and divide in half. Shape each half into a ball about 5 inches in diameter. Place each ball in the center of a greased 8-inch round cake pan. Cover and let rise in a warm place, free from draft, for about 1 hour or until doubled in bulk. Bake in 350-degree oven for 45 to 50 minutes or until done. Combine the cornstarch and 1/2 cup cold water in a saucepan. Bring to a boil over medium heat, stirring constantly. Cook, stirring constantly, for 1 minute. Brush over tops of loaves. Return bread to oven and bake for 2 to 3 minutes or longer until glaze is set. Remove from pans and cool on wire racks.

Photograph for this recipe on page 158.

SUGAR-CRISP ROLLS

2 to 2 1/2 c. unsifted flour	1/4 c. water
1 1/4 c. sugar	1/4 c. margarine
1/2 tsp. salt	1 egg, at room temperature
1 pkg. dry yeast	1 c. chopped pecans
1/4 c. milk	Melted margarine

Mix 3/4 cup flour, 1/4 cup sugar, salt and undissolved yeast thoroughly in a large bowl. Combine the milk, water and 1/4 cup margarine in a saucepan and place over low heat until liquids are warm. Margarine does not need to melt. Add to dry ingredients gradually and beat for 2 minutes with electric mixer at medium speed, scraping bowl occasionally. Add the egg and 1/4 cup flour, and beat at high speed for 2 minutes, scraping bowl occasionally. Stir in enough remaining flour to make a soft dough. Turn out onto a lightly floured board and knead for 8 to 10 minutes or until smooth and elastic. Cover and let rise in a warm place, free from draft, for about 1 hour or until doubled in bulk. Punch down and let rise for 30 minutes longer. Combine remaining sugar and pecans. Punch dough down. Turn out onto a lightly floured board and roll out to a 9 x 18-inch rectangle. Brush with melted margarine and sprinkle with half the sugar mixture. Roll up from long side as for jelly roll and seal edges. Cut into 1-inch slices. Roll each slice of dough into a 4-inch circle, using remaining sugar mixture in place of flour on board and coating both sides with sugar mixture. Place on greased baking sheets. Cover and let rise in a warm place, free from draft, for about 30 minutes or until doubled in bulk. Bake in 375-degree oven for 10 to 15 minutes or until done. Remove from baking sheets and cool on wire racks. 1 1/2 dozen.

Photograph for this recipe on page 158.

SCOTCH SHORTBREAD

1 c. butter	2 c. sifted all-purpose flour
1/2 c. confectioners' sugar	

Cream the butter in a bowl and beat in sugar gradually. Add the flour and mix well. Turn out on a baking sheet and pat into a circle about 7 inches in diameter. Pinch around edge of cake and prick all over with a fork. Chill for 30 minutes. Bake at 375 degrees for 5 minutes. Reduce temperature to 300 degrees and bake for 45 minutes longer or until golden. Cut in small wedges. Do not substitute margarine or shortening for butter.

Mrs. A. C. James, Springfield, Louisiana

SWEDISH STREUSEL-FILLED COFFEE CAKE

2 c. flour	Pinch of salt
3 tsp. baking powder	1 c. (packed) brown sugar
1/4 c. shortening	2 tsp. cinnamon
3/4 c. sugar	2 tbsp. melted butter
1 egg	1/2 c. chopped nuts
3/4 c. milk	

Sift the flour and baking powder together into a bowl and cut in shortening with a pastry blender. Add the sugar and mix well. Add egg, milk and salt and mix thoroughly. Pour half the batter into a greased 8 x 12-inch baking pan. Combine remaining ingredients for filling and mix well. Sprinkle half the filling on batter. Add remaining batter and top with remaining filling. Bake in 375-degree oven for 30 minutes.

Mrs. Berline R. Baldwin, Clarkton, North Carolina

TAHITIAN COFFEE CAKE

1 8-oz. can crushed pineapple	1/4 c. warm water
1/2 c. (firmly packed) light	1 pkg. yeast
brown sugar	1/2 c. sugar
3/4 c. margarine	1/2 tsp. salt
1 tsp. cinnamon	3 eggs, beaten
1 tsp. light corn syrup	1/4 c. milk
1/2 c. shredded coconut	2 c. unsifted flour
2 1/2 c. banana slices	

Combine the undrained pineapple, brown sugar, 1/4 cup margarine, cinnamon and corn syrup in a saucepan and bring to a boil over medium heat. Spoon into a 9-inch square pan. Sprinkle with coconut and top with banana slices. Pour the water into a small, warm bowl. Add the yeast and stir until dissolved. Cream remaining margarine with sugar and salt in a bowl. Add eggs, milk and yeast and beat until well blended. Stir in the flour and spoon over pineapple mixture carefully. Let rise in a warm place, free from draft, for about 1 hour or until doubled in bulk. Bake at 375 degrees for about 40 minutes or until done. Let stand in pan for 15 minutes, then invert over cake plate.

traditional
holiday
breads

When it's holiday time in America's Southland, the towns and villages are virtually filled with the smell of baking bread as homemakers celebrate the occasion with their families' favorite foods. Some of the most flavor-filled of these breads are those of foreign origin — the great holiday breads of half a hundred nations, adapted by southern homemakers for American palates.

Browse through the Southland's favorite holiday bread recipes now, in the pages that follow. Offer your family Easter's traditional breads — Angel Biscuits, Easter Basket Bread, and, of course, Hot Cross Buns. Each of these time-honored favorites will say "happy holiday" in its own special way.

When the end of the year approaches and Thanksgiving and Christmas loom on the horizon, why not share the products of these recipes with your friends and family? Few gifts are as appreciated as a loaf of homemade bread! Celebrate Thanksgiving with Cranberry Bread or Pumpkin Muffins — they make great gifts, too. The recipes for these breads — and more — are in this section.

All these savory breads are so delicious, you'll want to serve them year-round. In fact, why not prepare one now — and enjoy the acclaim of your surprised and happy family!

175

ANGEL BISCUITS

1 pkg. yeast	1 tsp. salt
1 c. warm water	4 tsp. baking powder
4 c. flour	1 c. shortening
1/4 c. sugar	1 c. buttermilk
1 tsp. soda	Melted butter

Dissolve the yeast in warm water. Sift the flour, sugar, soda, salt and baking powder together into a bowl and cut in shortening. Add the yeast and buttermilk and stir until mixed. Turn out onto a floured surface and knead lightly. Roll out and cut with a biscuit cutter. Dip in butter and place on a baking sheet. Let rise for 2 hours. Bake at 425 degrees for 12 to 15 minutes. Dough may be covered and refrigerated for 1 week.

Mrs. Bentley Rawdon, Jackson, Tennessee

CARROT LOAF

1 1/2 c. flour	1/4 c. chopped pecans
1 tsp. baking powder	1 c. sugar
1 tsp. soda	2/3 c. corn oil
1 tsp. cinnamon	2 eggs
1/4 tsp. salt	1/2 tsp. vanilla
1/2 c. seedless raisins	1 1/2 c. grated carrots

Sift the flour, baking powder, soda, cinnamon and salt together. Mix the raisins and pecans and dredge with 2 tablespoons flour mixture. Mix the sugar and oil in a bowl until blended, then beat in the eggs and vanilla. Add the flour mixture and carrots and mix well. Stir in the raisin mixture and turn into a greased 9 x 5 x 3-inch pan. Bake at 350 degrees for 1 hour to 1 hour and 10 minutes. Cool in pan on a rack. 6-8 servings.

Mrs. Tom Johnston, Atlanta, Georgia

EASTER BASKET BREAD

1 pkg. dry yeast	4 to 4 1/2 c. sifted flour
1 pkg. lemon pudding mix	4 eggs, beaten
1/4 c. margarine, or shortening	6 whole eggs in shell
1/2 tsp. salt	Candy decorettes
3/4 c. milk, scalded	

Dissolve the yeast in 1/4 cup warm water. Mix the pudding mix, margarine and salt in a bowl. Add the milk and stir until well mixed and butter is melted. Cool to lukewarm. Add 1 1/2 cups flour and mix well. Stir in the yeast and 3 beaten eggs and beat well. Add enough remaining flour gradually to make a soft dough. Turn out on a lightly floured surface and knead for 8 to 10 minutes or until smooth and elastic. Place in a greased bowl and turn to grease surface. Cover and let rise for 1 hour and 15 minutes or until doubled in bulk. Punch down and let rise again for about 1 hour or until doubled in bulk. Turn out on a lightly floured surface and divide into 3 parts. Form in balls. Cover and let rest for 10 minutes. Shape each part into a strand 20 inches long, then braid. Fit into a greased 10-inch round cake pan. Tuck the uncooked whole eggs into braid until almost covered. Cover and let rise for 45 minutes or until doubled in bulk. Mix remaining beaten egg and 1 tablespoon water and brush on loaf, then sprinkle with decorettes. Bake in 375-degree oven for 25 to 30 minutes or until done. The whole eggs may be colored with Easter egg dye before placing in braid, if desired.

Mrs. Lindy Mann, Aiken, South Carolina

ASCENSION THURSDAY LOAVES

1 c. warm potato water	1 tsp. salt
2 pkg. yeast	2 eggs, beaten
1/4 c. lukewarm mashed potatoes	1/2 c. melted margarine, cooled
8 tbsp. sugar	2 c. dark seedless raisins
5 1/4 c. (about) unsifted flour	

Pour the potato water into a large, warm bowl. Sprinkle with yeast and stir until dissolved. Add the mashed potatoes, 2 tablespoons sugar and 1 cup flour and beat until smooth. Cover and let rise for 30 minutes or until bubbly. Stir down. Add remaining sugar, salt and 1 cup flour and beat until smooth. Stir in the eggs, margarine and raisins. Add enough remaining flour to make a soft dough and mix well. Turn out on a lightly floured board and knead for about 5 minutes or until smooth and elastic. Place in a greased bowl and turn to grease top. Cover and let rise in a warm place, free from draft, for about 1 hour or until doubled in bulk. Punch down. Turn out onto a lightly floured board and divide in half. Let rest for 5 minutes. Shape each half into a loaf and place each in a greased 9 x 5 x 3-inch loaf pan. Cover and let rise in a warm place, free from draft, for about 40 minutes or until doubled in bulk. Bake in 350-degree oven for 40 minutes or until done. Warm water may be substituted for potato water.

HOT CROSS BUNS

1 pkg. yeast	2 eggs, beaten
Butter	7 to 7 1/2 c. flour
1/2 c. sugar	1 c. currants
1 tsp. salt	Confectioners' sugar icing
1 c. evaporated milk	

Dissolve the yeast in 1/2 cup warm water. Combine 1/4 cup butter, sugar and salt in a large bowl. Pour in 1 cup boiling water and stir until butter is melted. Add the milk and cool to lukewarm. Add yeast, eggs and 4 cups flour and beat until smooth. Add enough remaining flour to make a soft dough, then stir in the currants. Shape into a ball and place in a greased bowl. Turn to grease top. Cover and let rise until doubled in bulk. Punch down and shape into buns. Place on a greased baking sheet and cut a cross in top of each bun with a sharp knife. Cover and let rise until doubled in bulk. Bake at 450 degrees for 15 minutes. Brush tops of buns with butter. Cool, then outline crosses with confectioners' sugar icing.

Mrs. Mary Melton, Wytheville, Virginia

EASTER RAISIN BREAD

1/2 c. sugar	4 eggs
1/2 c. butter	1 tsp. salt
1 1/4 c. milk, scalded	1 tbsp. grated orange rind
2 pkg. yeast	1 tbsp. grated lemon rind
5 c. flour	1 c. seedless raisins

Place the sugar and butter in a large bowl. Add the milk and stir until sugar is dissolved and butter is melted. Cool to lukewarm. Add the yeast and stir until dissolved. Add 2 1/2 cups flour and beat until smooth. Combine the eggs and salt and beat well. Stir into the yeast mixture. Add remaining flour, orange rind, lemon rind and raisins and stir until mixed. Cover and let rise until doubled in bulk. Punch down and place in 2 greased loaf pans. Let rise until doubled in bulk. Bake at 350 degrees for 45 minutes.

Mrs. Don Borst, Laurel, Mississippi

EASTER BREAD

3/4 c. milk	1/2 c. warm water
3/4 c. potato water	7 to 8 c. flour
1 c. butter or margarine	1 c. mashed potatoes
2/3 c. sugar	3 eggs, beaten
2 tsp. salt	Raisins to taste (opt.)
2 pkg. dry yeast	

Mix the milk and potato water in a saucepan and heat until scalded. Add butter, sugar and salt and cool to lukewarm. Sprinkle yeast over warm water and let stand for 10 minutes. Sift 4 cups flour into a bowl. Add the milk mixture, potatoes, eggs and yeast and beat until smooth. Add enough remaining flour gradually to form a soft dough. Stir in raisins and knead on a floured surface until smooth. Place in a bowl and let rise for 1 hour in warm place. Shape into loaves and place in greased loaf pans. Let rise for 1 to 2 hours or until doubled in bulk. Bake in 400-degree oven for 10 minutes. Reduce temperature to 350 degrees and bake for 30 minutes longer or until brown. Dough may be refrigerated for 3 to 4 days before shaping into loaves.

Mrs. Carley Smith, Prattville, Alabama

CINNAMON ROLLS

1/2 c. shortening	1/4 c. lukewarm water
2 c. scalded milk	7 c. flour
2 eggs, beaten	1 c. seedless raisins
1 tsp. salt	1 c. chopped nuts
Sugar	Soft butter
1 c. mashed potatoes	Cinnamon
2 pkg. yeast	

Dissolve the shortening in the milk in a bowl and cool to lukewarm. Stir in the eggs, salt, 1 cup sugar and potatoes. Dissolve the yeast in lukewarm water, then stir into the potato mixture. Stir in the flour, raisins and nuts and mix thoroughly. Let rise until doubled in bulk. Roll out on a floured surface 1/2 inch thick and spread with butter. Sprinkle with sugar and cinnamon. Roll as for jelly roll and slice. Place, cut side up, in a well-greased baking pan and let rise until doubled in bulk. Bake at 350 degrees until golden brown. 5 dozen rolls.

Mrs. Agnes Carr, Laurel, Maryland

ORANGE ROLLS

1 1/4 c. scalded milk	2 eggs, well beaten
1/2 c. shortening	Grated orange peel
1 tsp. salt	3/8 c. orange juice
1/3 c. sugar	5 c. (about) flour
1 pkg. yeast	1 c. sifted powdered sugar

Combine the milk, shortening, salt and sugar in a bowl and cool to lukewarm. Add the yeast and stir until dissolved. Add eggs, 2 tablespoons orange peel and 1/4 cup orange juice and mix thoroughly. Add enough flour to form a soft dough and mix well. Cover and let stand for 10 minutes. Turn out on a lightly floured surface and knead until smooth and elastic. Place in a greased bowl and let rise in a warm place for about 2 hours or until doubled in bulk. Punch down. Roll out on a floured surface 1/2 inch thick and cut into 6 x 1/2-inch strips. Knot each strip and place on a greased baking sheet. Cover and let rise until doubled in bulk. Bake at 400 degrees for 15 minutes. Combine remaining orange juice, 1 teaspoon orange peel and powdered sugar and spread on rolls.

Mrs. Wanda Gray, Coosada, Alabama

THANKSGIVING RAISIN HARVEST COFFEE CAKE

1 1/2 c. sifted flour	2 c. finely chopped peeled
3 3/4 tsp. baking powder	cooking apples
1/2 tsp. salt	1 1/2 c. dark seedless raisins
3/4 c. sugar	2 lge. eggs, well beaten
3/4 c. butter	1 tbsp. milk

Sift the flour with baking powder, salt and sugar into a mixing bowl. Cut in the butter until mixture is consistency of fine bread crumbs. Stir in the apples and raisins. Add the eggs and milk and beat thoroughly. Batter will be very stiff. Spread in a well-greased 9-inch square pan and sprinkle generously with additional sugar. Bake in 350-degree oven for 55 to 60 minutes or until cake tests done. Cool slightly in pan before cutting. Serve warm with butter, if desired.

APPLE BREAD

1/2 c. butter	1 tsp. vanilla
1 c. sugar	2 c. flour, sifted
2 eggs	1 tsp. soda

| 1/2 tsp. salt | 1 c. chopped apples |
| 1/3 c. sour milk or orange juice | 1/3 c. chopped walnuts |

Cream the butter and sugar in a bowl. Add eggs and vanilla and beat well. Mix the flour, soda and salt and add to creamed mixture alternately with sour milk. Fold in the apples and walnuts and place in a greased loaf pan. Bake in 350-degree oven for about 55 minutes.

Mrs. Dean Holmes, Warner Robins, Georgia

MINCEMEAT COFFEE RINGS

3/4 c. milk, scalded	1/2 c. warm water
1/2 c. sugar	1 egg, beaten
2 tsp. salt	4 c. flour
1/2 c. margarine	1 lge. jar mincemeat
2 pkg. yeast	

Mix the milk, sugar, salt and margarine in a mixing bowl and cool to lukewarm. Dissolve the yeast in water, then stir into milk mixture. Add the egg and 2 cups flour and beat until smooth. Add remaining flour and blend well. Cover and refrigerate for at least 2 hours or overnight. Divide into 2 parts and roll each part out on a floured surface into a rectangle. Spread with mincemeat and roll as for jelly roll. Place rolls in a circle in greased round 9-inch cake pans, pressing ends together. Cut 4 slashes on top of each circle. Cover and let rise in a warm place until doubled in bulk. Bake at 350 degrees for about 30 minutes, then cool. Frost with confectioners' sugar frosting, if desired.

Kar Lynn Roberts, Pine Bluff, Arkansas

PUMPKIN MUFFINS

1 c. sifted flour	1/4 c. butter
3/4 c. sugar	1 egg, beaten
2 tsp. baking powder	1/2 c. canned pumpkin
1/2 tsp. cinnamon	1/2 c. evaporated milk
1/2 tsp. nutmeg	1/2 c. seedless raisins
1/4 tsp. salt	

Sift the flour, 1/2 cup sugar, baking powder, cinnamon, nutmeg and salt together into a medium mixing bowl. Cut in the butter until mixture resembles cornmeal. Combine the egg, pumpkin, milk and raisins. Add to flour mixture and stir just until mixed. Fill greased muffin cups 2/3 full and sprinkle 1/4 teaspoon sugar over each muffin. Bake in 400-degree oven for 20 to 25 minutes or until brown. 16 muffins.

Mrs. Ralph Houston, Frankfort, Kentucky

CRANBERRY BREAD

2 c. flour
1/2 tsp. soda
2 tbsp. butter
1 c. sugar
1 egg

1/2 tsp. salt
3/4 c. orange juice
1 c. chopped cranberries
1/2 c. chopped walnuts

Sift the flour and soda together. Cream the butter and sugar in a bowl, then beat in the egg and salt. Add the flour mixture alternately with orange juice, mixing well after each addition. Fold in the cranberries and walnuts and turn into a greased loaf pan. Bake at 350 degrees for 1 hour.

Mrs. R. L. Jones, Atlanta, Georgia

TOMATO BREAD

2/3 c. malted cereal granules
1 1/3 c. milk, scalded
1/4 c. melted shortening
2 eggs, well beaten
1 c. chopped fresh tomatoes

2 1/4 c. sifted flour
3/4 c. sugar
3 tsp. baking powder
1 1/2 tsp. salt

Preheat oven to 375 degrees. Place the cereal in a bowl and pour the milk over cereal. Cool. Stir in the shortening, eggs and tomatoes. Sift the flour, sugar, baking powder and salt together. Add the flour mixture and mix only enough to moisten dry ingredients. Turn into a greased 9 x 5 x 3-inch loaf pan. Bake for about 50 minutes or until bread tests done. Cool in pan on a rack for 10 minutes, then turn bread onto rack to cool completely. Wrap in plastic wrap and cool overnight before slicing.

Mrs. Leon P. Smith, Port Arthur, Texas

CHRISTMAS ORANGE BREAD

1/2 c. shortening
3/4 c. sugar
3 eggs
1/2 c. mashed bananas
1/2 c. orange juice
2 1/2 c. sifted flour

4 tsp. baking powder
3/4 tsp. salt
1 1/2 c. mixed candied fruit
1/4 c. raisins
3/4 c. chopped nuts

Cream the shortening in a mixing bowl. Add the sugar and beat until light and fluffy. Add eggs, one at a time, beating well after each addition. Combine bananas and orange juice. Sift the flour with baking powder and salt and mix in the candied fruit, raisins and nuts. Add to creamed mixture alternately with banana mixture and pour into greased and waxed paper-lined 9 x 5 x 3-inch loaf pan. Bake at 350 degrees for 1 hour or until done. Cool for about 20 minutes, then turn out on a rack.

Mrs. Mozelle B. Batchelor, Nashville, North Carolina

CHRISTMAS STOLLEN

2 pkg. yeast	6 eggs, beaten
1 lb. seedless raisins	1 1/2 c. melted butter
1 lb. currants	3 tbsp. lemon juice
11 c. flour	1 tsp. grated lemon peel
3/4 c. sugar	3 tbsp. cognac
1/2 tsp. salt	1/4 lb. chopped blanched
1/2 tsp. cinnamon	almonds
1/2 tsp. mace	1/2 lb. finely chopped citron
2 c. milk	1/2 c. confectioners' sugar

Dissolve the yeast in 1/2 cup lukewarm water. Combine the raisins and currants in a bowl and cover with boiling water. Let stand for 5 minutes, then drain. Rinse and drain again. Sift the flour, sugar, salt and spices together into a large bowl. Add the milk, eggs, 1 1/4 cups melted butter, lemon juice, lemon peel, 1 tablespoon cognac and yeast and stir until well mixed. Add the almonds, citron and raisin mixture and mix well. Cover the bowl and let stand in a warm place for 12 hours. Turn out onto a lightly floured surface and knead lightly. Divide in 2 parts. Shape each part into a crescent and place on a greased cookie sheet. Cover and let rise until doubled in bulk. Bake at 350 degrees for 1 hour, then cool. Mix remaining butter, remaining cognac and confectioners' sugar until smooth and frost loaves.

Mrs. James Egan, Ormond Beach, Florida

HOLIDAY BREAD

2 pkg. yeast	1 c. seedless raisins
1/2 c. sugar	1/2 c. chopped toasted almonds
2 tsp. salt	7 2/3 c. sifted flour
2/3 c. instant nonfat dry milk	3 c. sifted powdered sugar
2 eggs	I tsp. lemon juice
1/2 c. soft shortening	1 tsp. grated lemon rind
1/2 tsp. yellow food coloring	

Dissolve the yeast in 1/2 cup lukewarm water in a large bowl. Add the sugar, salt, dry milk, eggs, shortening, 1 1/2 cups water, food coloring, raisins and almonds and mix well. Stir in half the flour. Add remaining flour and mix well. Turn onto a lightly floured board and knead until smooth and elastic. Place in a greased bowl and turn to grease top. Cover with waxed paper, then with a towel. Let rise in a warm place for 45 minutes or until doubled in bulk. Punch down and let rise again until almost doubled in bulk. Punch down. Divide into 4 portions and form into balls. Place in 4 well-greased 1-pound coffee cans and let rise until doubled in bulk. Place cans on a cookie sheet. Bake at 375 degrees for 40 minutes or until brown. Cut around sides of cans gently with a knife. Remove from cans and place on a wire rack. Blend the powdered sugar, 3 tablespoons water, lemon juice and grated rind in a 1 1/2-quart bowl. Drizzle over tops of loaves while warm, allowing glaze to drip over sides. Sprinkle with colored decorettes, if desired.

Mrs. R. L. Berry, Little Rock, Arkansas

CHRISTMAS COFFEE RING

2 c. sifted all-purpose flour
3 tsp. baking powder
1 tsp. salt
2 tbsp. sugar
6 tbsp. butter or margarine
1/2 c. (about) milk
1 egg, beaten

1/4 c. softened butter or
   margarine
1/2 c. (packed) brown sugar
1 tbsp. cinnamon
1 tsp. allspice
1/2 c. raisins
1/2 c. chopped nuts

Sift the flour, baking powder, salt and sugar together into a bowl and cut in the butter until mixture resembles coarse meal. Add enough milk to the egg to make 3/4 cup liquid. Add all at once to the flour mixture and stir just until the flour is moistened. Turn out onto a lightly floured pastry cloth and knead gently for about 30 seconds. Roll to 9 x 12-inch rectangle and spread with the softened butter. Combine remaining ingredients except icing and sprinkle over dough to about 1 inch from edges. Roll as for jelly roll and place, seam side down, on a greased baking sheet to form a ring. Cut through ring with scissors almost to center at intervals and turn each slice slightly to side. Bake in 425-degree oven for 15 to 20 minutes or until browned. Frost with confectioners' sugar icing while warm.

CHRISTMAS MORNING COFFEE CAKE

1/2 c. shortening
3/4 c. sugar

1 tsp. vanilla
3 eggs

2 c. flour
1 tsp. baking powder
1 tsp. soda
1/2 pt. sour cream

1/2 c. butter
1 c. (packed) brown sugar
2 tsp. cinnamon
1 c. chopped walnuts

Cream the shortening with sugar and vanilla in a bowl. Add the eggs, one at a time, beating well after each addition. Sift the flour, baking powder and soda together and add to creamed mixture alternately with sour cream. Blend the butter, brown sugar, cinnamon and walnuts in a bowl. Pour half the batter into a greased tube pan and add half the brown sugar mixture. Repeat layers. Bake at 350 degrees for 50 minutes, then cool. Drizzle with confectioners' sugar icing, if desired. 8 servings.

Mrs. Larry Wheelis, Sarasota, Florida

HOLIDAY CRANBERRY-ORANGE BREAD

1 c. fresh cranberries
2 c. sifted all-purpose flour
1 1/4 c. sugar
1/4 c. instant mashed potato
   granules
2 tsp. baking powder
1 tsp. soda
1/2 tsp. salt

2 eggs, beaten
1/2 c. water
1/3 c. orange juice
3 tbsp. melted butter or
   margarine
1 tbsp. grated orange peel
1 c. chopped pecans

Cut the cranberries in halves. Sift the flour, sugar, potato granules, baking powder, soda and salt together into a bowl. Combine the eggs, water, orange juice, butter and orange peel. Add to the flour mixture and beat just until blended. Fold in the pecans and cranberries and pour into a greased 9 x 5 x 3-inch loaf pan. Bake in 350-degree oven for 1 hour to 1 hour and 10 minutes. Garnish with whole almonds, if desired.

Photograph for this recipe on page 174.

MERRY MINCE TEA BREAD

2 1/4 c. all-purpose flour
1/2 c. sugar
3 tsp. baking powder
1/2 tsp. salt
1 c. milk
1/4 c. salad oil

1 egg
1 c. mincemeat
1/4 c. chopped maraschino
   cherries
1/4 c. chopped nuts

Combine the flour, sugar, baking powder and salt in a mixing bowl. Combine the milk, oil and egg in a bowl and blend with a rotary beater. Stir in the mincemeat, cherries and nuts. Add to flour mixture and stir just until mixed. Turn into a greased 9 x 5 x 3-inch loaf pan. Bake at 350 degrees for about 1 hour and 10 minutes or until bread tests done. Cool for 10 minutes before removing from pan. Wrap in plastic wrap or waxed paper and let stand overnight before slicing.

Mrs. J. C. Pouncey, Chattanooga, Tennessee

CHANUKAH POTATO LATKES

6 potatoes, peeled	Salt and pepper to taste
1 onion, peeled	1/2 loaf bread
3 eggs	Flour
3 tsp. baking powder	Oil

Grate the potatoes and onion and strain, leaving small amount of liquid. Place in a bowl. Add the eggs, baking powder, salt and pepper and mix well. Remove crusts from bread and soak in just enough water to cover. Squeeze moisture from bread. Add the bread to potato mixture and mix well. Add enough flour to thicken and mix. Drop from large tablespoon into deep, hot oil and cook until brown on both sides. 40 latkes.

Esther Abelman, San Antonio, Texas

SHAVUOS SOUR CREAM COFFEE CAKE

1 stick butter or margarine	1/4 tsp. salt
1 c. sugar	1 tsp. baking powder
2 eggs	1 tsp. soda
1 1/3 c. sour cream	Cinnamon Topping
1 1/2 tsp. vanilla	Chopped nuts to taste
1 1/2 c. flour	

Cream the butter and sugar in a bowl. Add eggs and beat well. Mix the sour cream and vanilla. Sift the flour, salt, baking powder and soda together and add to creamed mixture alternately with the sour cream mixture. Pour half the batter into a well-greased and floured tube pan and sprinkle with half the Cinnamon Topping. Add remaining batter and swirl through batter with a knife. Add remaining Cinnamon Topping and sprinkle with chopped nuts. Bake at 350 degrees for 45 minutes.

Cinnamon Topping

1/3 c. sugar	1/4 c. grated orange peel
2 tsp. cinnamon	

Mix all ingredients in a bowl.

Mrs. Ben Switzer, Memphis, Tennessee

PASSOVER ALMOND-FRUIT KUGEL

1/2 c. dried apricots	3 eggs, separated
2 c. boiling water	2/3 c. sugar
2/3 c. blanched whole almonds	1/4 tsp. salt
1 8 1/2-oz. can crushed	1/4 tsp. cinnamon
pineapple	Tinted confectioners' icing
3 6 x 6-in. matzos	

Cut the apricots in halves and place in a saucepan. Add the boiling water. Cook until tender, then drain, reserving water. Reserve 5 almonds and chop remaining almonds fine. Drain the pineapple and reserve syrup. Place the matzos in a shallow pan and pour the reserved water and syrup over matzos. Let stand for 5 minutes, then squeeze almost dry. Beat the egg yolks in a bowl until light. Add the sugar, salt, cinnamon, matzos, fruits and chopped almonds. Beat the egg whites until stiff and fold into the egg yolk mixture. Turn into a warm, well-greased 1-quart casserole. Bake in 350-degree oven for 45 to 50 minutes or until well browned and firm in center of top. Cool for 10 minutes, then invert onto a plate. Drizzle with icing and garnish with reserved almonds. 5-6 servings.

PASSOVER MUFFINS

1 tsp. salt	2 c. matza meal
2 tbsp. sugar	1/2 c. melted shortening
1 1/2 c. boiling water	4 eggs

Dissolve the salt and sugar in the boiling water. Pour over the matza meal in a bowl and mix well. Let stand for 5 minutes. Add the shortening and eggs and mix thoroughly. Form into patties about 3/4 inch thick and 2 1/2 inches in diameter. Grease muffin cups with additional shortening and place patties in muffin cups. Bake at 450 to 475 degrees for 20 to 25 minutes. 12 muffins.

Mrs. Jack Ginsburg, Lakeland, Florida

ABBREVIATIONS USED IN THIS BOOK

Cup	c.	Large	lge.
Tablespoon	tbsp.	Package	pkg.
Teaspoon	tsp.	Small	sm.
Pound	lb.	Dozen	doz.
Ounce	oz.	Pint	pt.

MEASUREMENTS

3 tsp. = 1 tbsp.

2 tbsp. = 1/8 c.

4 tbsp. = 1/4 c.

8 tbsp. = 1/2 c.

16 tbsp. = 1 c.

5 tbsp. + 1 tsp. = 1/3 c.

12 tbsp. = 3/4 c.

4 oz. = 1/2 c.

8 oz. = 1 c.

16 oz. = 1 lb.

1 oz. = 2 tbsp. fat or liquid

2 c. fat = 1 lb.

2 c. = 1 pt.

2 c. sugar = 1 lb.

5/8 c. = 1/2 c. + 2 tbsp.

7/8 c. = 3/4 c. + 2 tbsp.

2 2/3 c. powdered sugar = 1 lb.

2 2/3 c. brown sugar = 1 lb.

4 c. sifted flour = 1 lb.

1 lb. butter = 2 c. or 4 sticks

2 pts. = 1 qt.

1 qt. = 4 c.

A few grains = less than 1/8 tsp.

Pinch = as much as can be taken between tip of finger and thumb

Speck = less than 1/8 tsp.

SUBSTITUTIONS

1 tablespoon cornstarch (for thickening) = 2 tablespoons flour (approximately)

1 cup sifted all-purpose flour = 1 cup plus 2 tablespoons sifted cake flour

1 cup sifted cake flour = 1 cup minus 2 tablespoons sifted all-purpose flour

1 teaspoon baking powder = 1/4 teaspoon baking soda plus 1/2 teaspoon cream of tartar

1 cup bottled milk = 1/2 cup evaporated milk plus 1/2 c. water

1 cup sour milk = 1 cup sweet milk into which 1 tablespoon vinegar or lemon juice has been stirred; or 1 cup buttermilk

1 cup sweet milk = 1 cup sour milk or buttermilk plus 1/2 teaspoon baking soda

1 cup cream, sour, heavy = 1/3 cup butter and 2/3 cup milk in any sour-milk recipe

1 cup cream, sour, thin = 3 tablespoons butter and 3/4 cup milk in sour-milk recipe

1 cup molasses = 1 cup honey

INDEX

PHOTOGRAPHY CREDITS: Standard Brands Products: Fleischmann's Yeast, Fleischmann's Margarine, Planter's Nuts, Blue Bonnet Margarine; General Foods Kitchens; United Fresh Fruit and Vegetable Association; Florida Citrus Commission; Apple Pantry: Washington State Apple Commission; Keith Thomas Company; California Raisin Advisory Board; Pillsbury Company; Quaker Oats Company; Pineapple Growers Association; The Pie Filling Institute; DIAMOND Walnut Growers, Inc.; North American Blueberry Council; Evaporated Milk Association; National Peanut Council; National Dairy Council; California Apricots Advisory Board; National Cherry Growers and Industries Foundation; Gerber Products Company; Ocean Spray Cranberries, Inc.; Pet, Inc.; C & H Sugar Kitchen; Green Giant Company; The R. T. French Company; Armour and Company.

Printed in the United States of America.